Prescription
Pain Relievers

TITLES IN THE *UNDERSTANDING DRUGS* SERIES

UNDERSTANDING DRUGS

Prescription Pain Relievers

MARY HARWELL SAYLER

CONSULTING EDITOR
DAVID J. TRIGGLE, PH.D.
University Professor
School of Pharmacy and Pharmaceutical Sciences
State University of New York at Buffalo

CHELSEA HOUSE
PUBLISHERS
An imprint of Infobase Publishing

PRESCRIPTION PAIN RELIEVERS

Chelsea House
An imprint of Infobase Publishing
132 West 31st Street
New York NY 10001

Library of Congress Cataloging-in-Publication Data

Sayler, Mary Harwell.
  Prescription pain relievers / Mary Harwell Sayler ; consulting editor,
David J. Triggle. — 1st ed.
    p. cm. — (Understanding drugs)
  Includes bibliographical references and index.
  ISBN-13: 978-1-60413-549-7 (hardcover : alk. paper)
  ISBN-10: 1-60413-549-2 (hardcover : alk. paper)   1. Analgesics—Juvenile
literature.   I. Triggle, D. J.   II. Title.   III. Series.
  RM319.S29 2010
  615'.783—dc22   2010024901

Text design by Kerry Casey
Cover design by Alicia Post
Composition by Newgen North America
Cover printed by Bang Printing, Brainerd, MN
Book printed and bound by Bang Printing, Brainerd, MN
Date printed: November 2010
Printed in the United States of America

10 9 8 7 6 5 4 3 2 1

This book is printed on acid-free paper.

All links and Web addresses were checked and verified to be correct at the time of publication. Because of the dynamic nature of the Web, some addresses and links may have changed since publication and may no longer be valid.

Contents

foreword

THE USE AND ABUSE OF DRUGS

For thousands of years, humans have used a variety of sources with which to cure their ills, cast out devils, promote their well-being, relieve their misery, and control their fertility. Until the beginning of the twentieth century, the agents used were all of natural origin, including many derived from plants as well as elements such as antimony, sulfur, mercury, and arsenic. The sixteenth-century alchemist and physician Paracelsus used mercury and arsenic in his treatment of syphilis, worms, and other diseases that were common at that time; his cure rates, however, remain unknown. Many drugs used today have their origins in natural products. Antimony derivatives, for example, are used in the treatment of the nasty tropical disease leishmaniasis. These plant-derived products represent molecules that have been "forged in the crucible of evolution" and continue to supply the scientist with molecular scaffolds for new drug development.

Our story of modern drug discovery may be considered to start with the German physician and scientist Paul Ehrlich, often called the father of chemotherapy. Born in 1854, Ehrlich became interested in the ways in which synthetic dyes, then becoming a major product of the German fine chemical industry, could selectively stain certain tissues and components of cells. He reasoned that such dyes might form the basis for drugs that could interact selectively with diseased or foreign cells and organisms. One of Ehrlich's early successes was development of the arsenical "606"—patented under the name *Salvarsan*—as a treatment for syphilis. Ehrlich's goal was to create a "magic bullet," a drug that would target only the diseased cell or the invading disease-causing organism and have no effect on healthy cells and tissues. In this he was not successful, but his great research did lay the groundwork for the successes of the twentieth century, including the discovery of the sulfonamides and the antibiotic penicillin. The latter agent saved countless lives during World War II. Ehrlich, like many scientists, was an optimist. On the eve of World War I, he wrote, "Now that the liability to, and danger of, disease are to a large extent circumscribed—the efforts of chemotherapeutics are directed as far as possible to fill up the gaps left in this ring." As we shall see in the pages of this volume, it is neither the first nor the last time that science has proclaimed its victory over nature, only to have to see this optimism dashed in the light of some freshly emerging infection.

From these advances, however, has come the vast array of drugs that are available to the modern physician. We are increasingly close to Ehrlich's magic bullet: Drugs can now target very specific molecular defects in a number of cancers, and doctors today have the ability to investigate the human genome to more effectively match the drug and the patient. In the next one to two decades, it is almost certain that the cost of "reading" an individual genome will be sufficiently cheap that, at least in the developed world, such personalized medicines will become the norm. The development of such drugs, however, is extremely costly and raises significant social issues, including equity in the delivery of medical treatment.

The twenty-first century will continue to produce major advances in medicines and medicine delivery. Nature is, however, a resilient foe. Diseases and organisms develop resistance to existing drugs, and new drugs must constantly be developed. (This is particularly true for anti-infective and anticancer agents.) Additionally, new and more lethal forms of existing infectious diseases can develop rapidly. With the ease of global travel, these can spread from Timbuktu to Toledo in less than 24 hours and become pandemics. Hence the current concerns with avian flu. Also, diseases that have previously been dormant or geographically circumscribed may suddenly break out worldwide. (Imagine, for example, a worldwide pandemic of Ebola disease, with public health agencies totally overwhelmed.) Finally, there are serious concerns regarding the possibility of man-made epidemics occurring through the deliberate or accidental spread of disease agents—including manufactured agents, such as smallpox with enhanced lethality. It is therefore imperative that the search for new medicines continue.

All of us at some time in our life will take a medicine, even if it is only aspirin for a headache or to reduce cosmetic defects. For some individuals, drug use will be constant throughout life. As we age, we will likely be exposed to a variety of medications—from childhood vaccines to drugs to relieve pain caused by a terminal disease. It is not easy to get accurate and understandable information about the drugs that we consume to treat diseases and disorders. There are, of course, highly specialized volumes aimed at medical or scientific professionals. These, however, demand a sophisticated knowledge base and experience to be comprehended. Advertising on television is widely available but provides only fleeting information, usually about only a single drug and designed to market rather than inform. The intent of this series of books, **Understanding Drugs**, is to provide the lay reader with intelligent, readable, and accurate descriptions of drugs, why and how they are used, their limitations, their side effects, and their future. The series will discuss both *"treatment drugs"*—typically, but not exclusively, prescription drugs, that have well-established criteria of both efficacy and safety—and *"drugs of abuse,"* agents that have pronounced pharmacological and physiological effects but that are, for a variety of reasons, not to be considered for therapeutic purposes. It is our hope that these books will provide readers with sufficient information to satisfy their immediate needs and to serve as an adequate base for further investigation and for asking intelligent questions of health care providers.

—David J. Triggle, Ph.D.
University Professor
School of Pharmacy and Pharmaceutical Sciences
State University of New York at Buffalo

1

Prescription Pain Relievers

ALL PAIN IS NOT THE SAME

Everyone feels **pain** at one time or another, but pain has many faces. **Acute pain** comes on suddenly, letting the person know something is wrong, but **chronic pain** goes on and on. Either type can affect people differently with the degree of discomfort ranging from an insignificant ache to a huge hurt, depending on the cause, how long the pain lasts, and the sensitivity of the nerves involved in an illness or injury.

Since pain is individually felt and therefore subjective, medical professionals try to help patients pinpoint pain and its severity. For instance, when a doctor, nurse, or therapist asks a patient to assess pain on a **numeric pain scale** from zero to ten, zero means no pain, one to three is mild pain, four to six is moderate, and seven to ten is severe pain. Ten represents the worst pain imaginable.

Sometimes the sensitivity or intensity of that discomfort has to do with location. For example, nerve endings closer to the surface of the skin might sense a sharp stab or an electric jolt, whereas nerves deeper in the body may bring on a dull ache. A medical professional will most likely ask the patient to point to the pain or touch the area that's hurting. In addition, the person will probably be asked to describe what the pain feels like. The larger a patient's vocabulary of descriptive words, the more clues a doctor will have to discern the cause of the pain, make an accurate diagnosis, determine what to do, and prescribe an appropriate medication or course of treatment. The more precise a patient can be in describing and locating pain, the more a physician will

A MINI-THESAURUS FOR DEGREES AND TYPES OF PAIN

Throbbing	Shooting	Stabbing
Stinging	Jolting	Aching
Tiring	Tingling	Binding
Nagging	Scorching	Squeezing
Nauseating	Excruciating	Sickening

know which medication to prescribe. And that's important because all pain relievers are not the same.

PAIN RELIEF DRUGS

The purpose of any prescription pain reliever is **pain management**. Successful pain management can enable a person to go to school or work, perform daily activities within sensible limits, and carry on a reasonably normal life. Excruciating pain can hinder that, but an appropriately prescribed prescription pain reliever (PPR) can help to restore a healthful quality of life.

Medications for pain relief come in two categories: **over-the-counter (OTC)** drugs (available without prescription) and **opioid analgesics** or **narcotics** (available only by prescription). For extra-strength relief, some OTC medications such as aspirin or another **nonsteroidal anti-inflammatory drug (NSAID)** may also be available in prescription strength.

Depending on the person's age and medical condition, the method for taking pain relievers can vary too. Usually NSAIDs such as aspirin, **ibuprofen,** ketoprofen, or naproxen come in pills, tablets, or capsules. Similarly, opioid **analgesics** may be prescribed as a tablet, capsule, or time-release pill. If, however, a patient cannot swallow a pill or needs an immediate method of receiving relief from excruciating pain, the doctor may prescribe a pain reliever in the form of a liquid, **suppository**, skin patch, or **buccal** tablet that dissolves in the mouth.

Besides these variations, one type of medication may relieve pain in one part of the body but not another. For instance, an athlete who has been injured may need pain relief for a torn muscle or broken bone, but this might not be the same medication prescribed to ease menstrual cramps, **migraine** headaches, or postsurgical pain. Why? Generally speaking, the chemical makeup of a medication acts on the body in a unique way, which will be discussed in Chapter 3.

Figure 1.1 Many teens abusing prescription pain relievers may simply take them from the family medicine cabinet.   *(© Photo Researchers, Inc.)*

Table 1.1 Opioid Analgesics	
Generic Name (example brand)	Conditions Treated and Methods of Use
buprenorphine (Buprenex)	Usually given in a tablet or by injection, this strong narcotic does not work well with other **opioids** but can provide pain relief by itself for up to eight hours. Therefore, the drug may be used to treat moderate to severe pain following surgery, or a skin patch may be prescribed to ease chronic bone, nerve, or cancer pain.
butorphanol (Stadol)	This strong opioid analgesic given in liquid form can help to boost the effects of anesthesia or relieve pain before and during surgery.
codeine and acetaminophen (Tylenol with codeine)	Also known as methylmorphine, a small amount of this rather mild pain reliever converts to morphine in the body but has only about one-tenth of its strength. Combining codeine with aspirin or Tylenol provides stronger pain relief than either drug alone. Often used to ease back pain or suppress a cough, this drug is a widely prescribed opioid.
fentanyl (Duragesic)	Highly subject to abuse, this strong opioid is administered through a slow-release skin patch to treat chronic pain of moderate to severe intensity.
fentanyl (Fentora)	This buccal tablet dissolves in the mouth, making it especially useful in treating breakthrough pain in cancer patients.
fentanyl (Sublimaze)	May be given in a lozenge to sedate children before potentially painful medical procedures. This strong opioid can also be injected or given with other pain medications before, during, or after surgery.
heroin (diamorphine)	This potent narcotic relieves pain for four or five hours, but its high potential for an **adverse event** or lethal **overdose** keeps the drug from having FDA approval for prescription use in the U.S.
hydrocodone bitartrate and acetaminophen (Vicodin)	Combining this narcotic with the less potent **acetaminophen** increases the strength of both in treating moderate to severe pain. Usually administered in tablet form, the drug may be used instead of codeine, for instance, to relieve a cough for eight to ten hours.
hydromorphone (Dilaudid)	This fast-acting substitute for morphine can be used to treat chronic pain or give quick relief by pill, injection, or suppository. Since its analgesic effect lasts only four to five hours, a time-release form may be prescribed for around-the-clock treatment.

Generic Name (example brand)	Conditions Treated and Methods of Use
levorphanol (Levo-Dromoran)	This potent drug, with pain-relieving action stronger than morphine, may be administered by injection or pill. Analgesic effects last about six hours.
meperidine hydrochloride (Demerol)	Used to treat moderate to severe pain, this analgesic drug works best in preventing pain rather than relieving it. For temporary treatment of pain after surgery or an injury, injections may be given every few hours during a short period of recuperation. Since the drug can cause such serious side effects as seizures and psychosis, doctors seldom prescribe it for long-term use.
methadone (Dolophine)	Similar to morphine in potency, this strong drug may be prescribed to ease chronic pain since it is relatively inexpensive and its effects can last for up to 48 hours. Unlike oxycodone, however, **methadone** has not been chemically engineered to h8 drug, so concentration levels in the blood may vary considerably between doses. Most often methadone is used to lessen the harsh symptoms of withdrawal during treatment of heroin or other drug **addiction**.
morphine (Astramorph)	This very potent narcotic provides powerful relief for chronic pain and fast relief for severe pain through a pill, liquid, or injection, but side effects or adverse events can be equally potent.
oxycodone (OxyContin)	Used instead of morphine, this strong narcotic often comes in a time-release form to treat severe or ongoing pain around the clock. Instead of lessening the sensation of pain, however, the drug increases the body's tolerance of pain. Sometimes oxycodone may be combined with aspirin or, as in the popular medication Percocet, with acetaminophen for an additional analgesic effect.
oxymorphone (Opana)	Similar to morphine, this strong opioid may be administered in a time-release pill, injection, or suppository to relieve severe or chronic pain but not immediately after surgery because of its high potential for **respiratory depression**.
pentazocine (Talwin)	To be taken only by mouth, this opioid analgesic can be lethal when misused, injected, or taken with other drugs. The narcotic has also been reported to cross the placental barrier and depress the **central nervous system** of a fetus. In treating pain the drug brings relief for about three hours. It is similar in strength to codeine but can cause anxiety and confusion in some patients.

(continues)

Table 1.1 (continued)	
Generic Name (example brand)	Conditions Treated and Methods of Use
propoxyphene (Darvon)	Used to relieve mild to moderate pain, this older medication is about as strong as an OTC drug such as aspirin, but it is addictive.
tramadol (Ultram)	Weaker than opiates, this **synthetic opioid** may be used to treat moderate pain and neuralgia or prescribed in time-release form for around-the-clock treatment. Some doctors believe the drug relieves anxiety disorders and depression.

Not all prescription pain relievers are opioids, but all opioids are narcotics. Derived from **opium** poppies, these drugs have the potential to become **addictive.** Therefore, doctors prescribe opioids cautiously, with a specific purpose and certain advantages in mind. For example, **morphine** may be used before or after surgery to lessen intense pain. **Codeine** might be used to treat less severe pain, and because of the potential **side effects, meperidine hydrochloride** might not be used at all.

Every year doctors write more than 100 million prescriptions for **opiate** analgesics, meaning these drugs are prescribed more often than any other medication. According to her testimony before a subcommittee of the U.S. House of Representatives, Dr. Nora D. Volkow of the National Institutes of Health reported that **oxycodone** and **hydrocodone** prescriptions more than doubled between 1994 and 2001.[1] Taking prescription pain medication at any time for any reason other than pain relief is a dangerous practice. Taken at specific times and in the specific doses prescribed for actual pain, however, PPRs can be beneficial for many people. According to the "pain" entry in *Taber's,* about 155 million Americans need pain relief each year.

ABUSE OF PRESCRIPTION PAIN RELIEVERS

Valid medical reasons put prescription pain medications in a bathroom medicine chest in the first place, but this is not the typical reason that adolescents, teens, and young adults take them out. According to a report titled

"Prescription Drug Abuse and Addiction" from the Director of the National Institute on Drug Abuse, 48 million people aged 12 and up have used prescription drugs for nonmedical reasons.[2] This represents about 20% of the entire population of the United States, with the causes for nonmedical use often varying by age group. For instance, elderly persons may take or be given more medications than needed because medical personnel have overprescribed or because the patient misunderstands the medication dosage and gets confused about the instructions that must be followed. Teenagers, however, typically have other nonmedical uses in mind. One in five adolescents[3] between 12 and 17 has abused prescription pain relievers. Some teens rummage through a medicine chest at home, while others may get pain medications from a friend. Although these teens usually know to stay away from street drugs, they might not know that drugs taken too often or taken for the wrong reasons can become dangerous and even deadly. For example, a PPR might be an opioid a surgeon prescribed to relieve intense pain for a short time after a surgical procedure, but long-term use of the same opium-derived medication could soon became addictive.

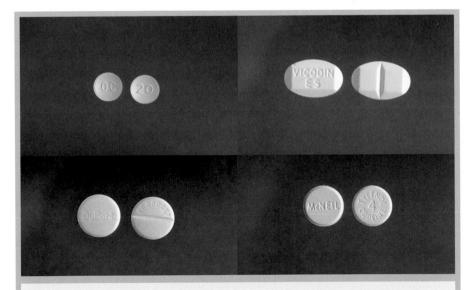

Figure 1.2 Commonly abused prescription pain relievers (clockwise from top left): oxycodone (OxyContin), hydrocodone (Vicodin), codeine with acetaminophen (Tylenol with codeine), and oxycodone and acetaminophen (Percocet). (Drug Enforcement Administration)

Combining drugs is also risky business. Teenagers who experiment with getting high by **pharming** or mixing medications they assume are safe may fall victim to **drug poisoning**. In 2004[4] alone at least 20,000 people died by accidentally poisoning themselves with drugs. Although more people died that same year in vehicular accidents, deaths from accidental drug poisoning outnumbered homicides in the United States. From 1999 to 2004, fatalities from **opioid analgesics** rose 160% in the United States, with more young people dying from prescription pain relievers than the total number of teens who overdosed on **heroin** and cocaine. A national survey reported in September 2008 that nonmedical use of PPRs went up another 12% during the previous year alone.[5]

FACTORS BEHIND PRESCRIPTION PAIN RELIEVER ABUSE

Numerous resources in the back of this book discuss many aspects of drug use, misuse, and abuse. All seem to agree that teenagers can be drawn to drugs for a variety of reasons. In addition to a legitimate use for physical pain, some teens try drugs to ease emotional pain, to experiment, or as a result of peer pressure.

Fitting into a group matters to most teenagers, but even more so to those who feel lonely, isolated, or socially inept. Students who are new to a community may be especially prone to use drugs as a quick way to connect with individuals or a group they consider to be popular, edgy, fun, daring, or generally well accepted by others at school.

Most teenagers experience times of feeling down, bored, or listless. Many just want to do something different to lessen monotony. Others wish their lives could be more exciting, bold, or adventurous. These teens seem most apt to experiment with drugs to feel a rush or get high even though living on the edge often means taking dangerous risks. Hanging out with kids who have easy access to PPRs and other drugs increases the likelihood of taking chances that teenagers might not otherwise consider.

Bright students and gifted athletes often feel heavy pressures at home and school to excel. For sensitive, talented teens who care a great deal about their family or future and want to do well in sports and school, PPR use may seem like an easy way to relax, lighten the stress, and feel less anxious about themselves and life.

Teens with low self-esteem and little family support or school interaction may be especially likely to self-medicate emotional or psychological pain with PPRs. Unfortunately, this is not the best way for teens to help themselves. Teens with social, emotional, or mental health problems need professional assistance and the help of compassionate adults who can help them to work through and resolve crucial issues.

WHAT DO DOCTORS RECOMMEND AND WHY?

Some patients may be given strong PPRs for **palliative care** in the later days or final stage of a terminal illness. In such instances the physician or medical staff will not be particularly concerned about potential for addiction but about making the patient as comfortable as possible. This is not always easy to do. For instance, patients who require drugs for any length of time often develop drug **tolerance**, which means that the medication no longer works as well to relieve pain. Therefore the dosage must be increased, the medication changed, or a new combination of drugs found.

Although those changes usually work toward more effective pain relief, side effects often increase too. For example, patients who use opioids of any kind may experience nausea, insomnia, breathing problems, sexual problems, and the inability to think clearly. The most common side effect of opioids is sluggish digestion that causes uncomfortable bouts of dryness and constipation. Increasing water intake can help to counteract this side effect. However, this and the other side effects just mentioned may give medical personnel cause to hesitate about prescribing more opioids.

Besides an ongoing concern for their patients, doctors also have to be concerned about legal issues affecting themselves and their own medical practice. As Dana Cassell reported in her book *The Encyclopedia of Death and Dying,* some state and local laws restrict the medical use of opioids to treat pain. The patient's insurance company may limit coverage of medications too, or object to covering additional pharmaceutical costs.

According to a report from the American Medical Association (AMA) titled "Standards, Laws, and Regulations Addressing Pain Medications and Medical Practice," approximately 75 million Americans report suffering from acute and chronic noncancer pain that is not adequately relieved. Why does this occur? The AMA explains that many diverse factors influence

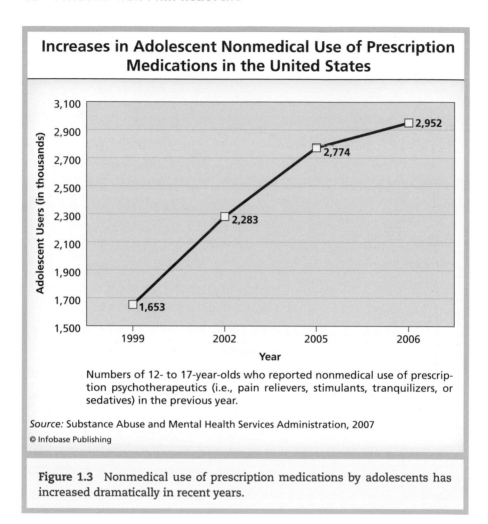

Increases in Adolescent Nonmedical Use of Prescription Medications in the United States

Numbers of 12- to 17-year-olds who reported nonmedical use of prescription psychotherapeutics (i.e., pain relievers, stimulants, tranquilizers, or sedatives) in the previous year.

Source: Substance Abuse and Mental Health Services Administration, 2007

© Infobase Publishing

Figure 1.3 Nonmedical use of prescription medications by adolescents has increased dramatically in recent years.

undertreatment, such as lack of medical training in managing pain or prescribing opioids and in understanding addiction and its side effects. Fear of overlooking governmental regulations presents a concern too. Since tolerance and **physical dependence** typically occur with extended drug use, physicians may have difficulty differentiating those consequences from addiction. Such misunderstandings influence how doctors make decisions and how patients accept a plan of pharmaceutical treatment.

2
History of Pain Relief Drugs

*Friedrich Wilhelm Sertürner shook his head over the dog lying lifeless before him. The young pharmacist had not wished to harm the gentle little creature. He had merely meant to see if the **extract** he obtained from opium would cause the dog to sleep, not die. Indeed the three other dogs he used for his experiment seemed fine once the heavy bouts of vomiting and convulsions had finally ceased.*

*Despite disappointing results during that first decade of the nineteenth century, the German-born Sertürner continued working with the poppy-derived opium and testing what he found. In 1817 he officially reported his success in extracting colorless crystals that would readily dissolve in **alcohol** or acid but not in water. Since Sertürner hoped to prove that these pure crystals had the same sleep-inducing effects as opium, he called the substance morphium or morphine in honor of Morpheus, the Greek god of dreams. He also continued his experiments, but not on dogs or a house mouse as he had done previously. This time Sertürner decided to try the drug on himself and three teenage boys.*

As he explained in his report, "In order to test my earlier experiments strictly, I encouraged three persons, none older than seventeen years, to take morphine with me simultaneously. Warned by the previous effects, however, I merely administered half a grain dissolved in half a drachma of alcohol and diluted with several ounces of distilled water."

No one fell asleep or even seemed drowsy as the pharmacist had hoped, but their eyes and cheeks flushed poppy red. About a half-hour later he gave everyone in the group another half-grain of the crystals, which greatly aggravated the redness and also produced headaches and nausea.

Sertürner reported, "After another 15 minutes, we swallowed another half-grain of morphium, undissolved, as a coarse powder, with 10 drops of alcohol and a half-ounce of water." Immediately the group experienced severe stomach pains, still without drowsiness but with such intense fatigue they all came close to fainting. Sertürner himself "fell into a dream-like state and sensed in the extremities, particularly the arms, a slight twitching which accompanied the pulse beats." Days went by before the side effects completely disappeared, and Sertürner noted, "Judging from these highly unpleasant experiences, I deduce that morphine, even in small quantities, acts as a strong poison."[1]

POPPIES

Long before the arrival of the Latin name *Papaver somniferum,* poppies were being cultivated in various places around the world to produce the opium from which other addictive narcotics such as morphine and heroin gradually blossomed into use. Archaeologists date the earliest fossilized poppy seeds to 30,000 B.C., citing them as proof that Neanderthals once used the poppy in one form or another. Whether the plants were cultivated and used prior to recorded history or not, archaeological studies and ancient documents show that poppy fields flourished in Persia, Mesopotamia, and other ancient civilizations about 4,000 B.C. For example, a Sumerian text recorded the first reference to poppies around 4,000 B.C., and an Egyptian papyrus text advised parents to use the concentrated juice of an unripe seedpod to curb excessive crying in children. Also in Egypt, the tombs of pharaohs have been found to contain opium artifacts.

In ancient Rome, street vendors sold opium, one of the narcotics derived from poppies, and Roman emperors used the drug. Indeed, ancient peoples around present-day Europe often ate poppy parts, sometimes for medicinal purposes. For instance, the renowned Greek surgeon Galen, who served as a physician to the gladiators, reported the poppy's ability to cure ailments ranging from poison and snakebite to chronic headache, deafness, melancholy, and "all pestilences."

Figure 2.1 Opiate drugs were derived at first from the opium poppy plant, seen here. At top, the plant (*Papaver somniferum*) is seen in full bloom. In the bottom view, sap is being taken out of the pod for use in making drugs.   (*©Photo Researchers, Inc. / © Corbis*)

Figure 2.2   San Francisco opium den in the early twentieth century.   *(Library of Congress)*

In mid-nineteenth century Asia, the Imperial Chinese court banned the use of opium, which Britain challenged, causing two conflicts known as the Opium Wars. When the Chinese lost both wars, the British forced them to open new ports to the poppy trade. By the end of that century, about one-fourth of the men in China had become addicted to opium.

Around Europe, Asia, and elsewhere, however, sculptors and artisans found artistic uses for poppy plants as they carved or painted images of poppy seeds and the perky red-orange poppy flowers with their little umbrella-striped center. In some areas of the Middle East today, mourners drink cool poppy tea at funerals, but in the United States, evidence of poppies can most be seen in the tiny blue-black poppy seeds in bird feeders or on top of salads, breadsticks, and rolls.

LAUDANUM

In the sixteenth century the German-Swiss pharmacist-physician Paracelsus combined opium with alcohol into the concoction known as **laudanum**. By the seventeenth century a well-respected English doctor, Thomas Sydenham, had begun prescribing the drug to treat medical conditions involving pain and lack of sleep. In the 1800s doctors used laudanum to ease the painful wounds

Figure 2.3 Laudanum bottles from the nineteenth century. *(© Getty Images)*

suffered by soldiers during war. Reportedly such well-known poets and writers as Charles Dickens and Elizabeth Barrett Browning used the tincture, too, choosing that discreet form of ingestion over the distasteful pipe that passed from person to person in an opium den. By the end of the nineteenth century genteel families had begun stocking laudanum on their medicine shelves at home.[2]

THE FLOWERING OF DRUG USE

Until the early twentieth century, the United States had no legal restrictions on narcotics. People could buy medicine from a pharmacy without a prescription, and there were no warning labels to tell them about the addictive potential of any narcotic. Even an infant might be given **paregoric**—a liquid combining opium, alcohol, water, and other ingredients intended to treat chronic colicky cries, an occasional upset stomach, or those achy gums during teething. Heroin, an opium-based drug now illegal in the United States, was once a primary ingredient in at least one over-the-counter cough remedy. More commonly, though, vials of laudanum and opium could be found for sale among food items and other products on the shelves of drugstores and grocery shops.

The invention of the **hypodermic** needle swiftly changed the way that individuals and society looked at medications and drug use. Instead of giving the body a gentle boost with a **tonic, herbal medicine**, or **elixir** as they had done for centuries past, physicians now discovered that an injection of opium or morphine would provide a fast and highly potent means of delivering **anesthesia** to control severe pain before, during, or even after surgery. Until then the medical community and society in general had considered most medicines and remedies as being helpful and **curative** rather than potentially harmful or addictive. For the most part that was true. However, the little black bags that doctors carried soon held a hypodermic needle to use (and likely reuse) as needed to administer a quick fix for severe pain. By the time the potential for addiction had been recognized as a hazard to health, opium-based drugs and hypodermic needles had slipped into recreational use.

GOVERNMENT DRUG REGULATION

For centuries doctors had mixed remedies from a fairly standard assortment of natural herbs and minerals until imitation flavorings, food colorings,

THE HYPODERMIC NEEDLE

The hypodermic needle with its plunging syringe caused drug use to increase quickly, but who first got that idea to work? According to Irish history, the Dublin-born doctor Francis Rynd detailed his invention of the hypodermic syringe in the *Dublin Medical Press* in 1845, eight years before Alexander Wood received credit for the same thing. Reportedly Dr. Rynd wanted to ease **neuralgia**, or intense nerve pain, in patients seeking treatment in Meath Hospital, a charitable institution built to serve the poor. After injecting various sedatives into the bloodstream of his hospitalized patients, Dr. Rynd reported that the most beneficial effects came through "a solution of morphia in creosote, ten grains of the former to one drachma of the latter."[3]

When opportune times, needs, or conditions coax people into exploring new ideas, greatly inventive minds often think alike. Not surprisingly, then, Scotland and France both claimed inventors of the hypodermic syringe in 1853 or shortly thereafter, when the Scottish doctor Alexander Wood and French doctor Charles-Gabriel Pravaz came up with similar devices. At about the same time, the American doctor Fordyce Barker introduced a needle as a means of delivering medication, but the term *hypodermic* most likely did not exist until Dr. Charles Hunter of London made up the word in 1858.[4]

Although debate continues as to who should properly receive credit for the hypodermic needle, Dr. Wood of Scotland may be the most renowned of this group of highly inventive mid-nineteenth-century doctors. Dr. Wood proved the powerful results of injecting morphine into the bloodstream, but he and his wife became addicted to the drug. Mrs. Wood went on to receive the regrettable distinction of becoming the first woman in recorded history to die of a **drug overdose** by an injection into a vein.[5]

preservatives, and other artificial ingredients changed or misrepresented the mix. Instead of the age-old concern about the actual healing properties of a medicine, a concoction now needed to look pretty, taste good, and have a unique claim to extol. The rise of newspapers, magazines, and flyers with plenty of space for advertisements also encouraged the sale of newly invented bottled tonics and elixirs.

Into this era of quack medicines and questionable cures, standards for known drugs were either low or nonexistent and the primary chemical ingredients often tainted or impure. In hope of solving this problem and curing the poor reputation of American-made medicines that relied on ingredients imported from other countries, Congress passed the Drug Importation Act in 1848, authorizing the U.S. Customs Service to stop impure drugs from coming across U.S. borders. As later explained in *FDA Consumer* magazine, "Opium was a vital painkiller, and when medical shipments arrived in New York, they had been cut to one-third natural strength and laced with Spanish anise and other bitter powders to disguise the dilution. Further, a substantial part of all opium shipments was infested with live worms." With few or no standards and government regulations, "The market in medicines . . . was essentially the same as the illicit trade today in heroin, cocaine, and other drugs. The supply was unreliable, the purity suspect, the price high and variable."[6]

By the late 1880s Dr. Harvey W. Wiley, known as the "Crusading Chemist," started campaigning for federal laws. Some years later, a number of physicians tried another approach, and in 1905 the American Medical Association (AMA) began requiring drug companies to prove the effectiveness of a product before they could advertise in the journal or other publications produced by the AMA.

In 1906 President Theodore Roosevelt signed the Pure Food and Drug Act, which, according to the U.S. Food and Drug Administration (FDA), was the first of more than 200 public health and consumer protection laws. Initially those laws aimed toward protecting people from impure foods and misleading labels rather than addictive or harmful drugs. For example, such products as substandard tea and such processes as substandard meatpacking came under the watchful eye of the FDA. In 1911, however, the U.S. Supreme Court ruled that the 1906 Pure Food and Drug Act did not prohibit false therapeutic claims, but only false and misleading statements about the ingredients or identity of a drug. Therefore, the following year Congress passed the Sherley Amendment to stop the practice of labeling medicines with false therapeutic claims intended to defraud the purchaser.

Although the 1906 Pure Food and Drug Act was not revised until the 1930s, the Harrison Narcotic Act of 1914 mandated "prescriptions for products

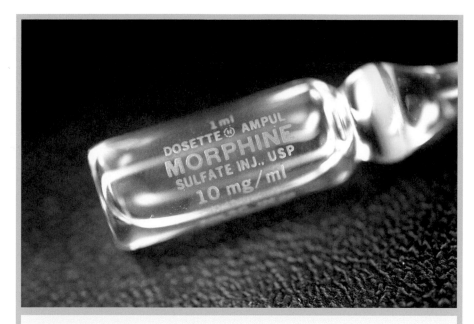

Figure 2.4 Morphine is a very potent narcotic that provides powerful relief for chronic pain and fast relief for severe pain. *(©Photo Researchers, Inc.)*

exceeding the allowable limit of narcotics and . . . increased record-keeping for physicians and pharmacists who dispense narcotics." In 1938 Congress passed the Federal Food, Drug, and Cosmetic (FDC) Act, which, among other things, required new drugs to be proven safe before marketing. This began a new system of drug regulation. In 1970 the Comprehensive Drug Abuse Prevention and Control Act called for categorization of "drugs based on abuse and addiction potential compared to their therapeutic value." More reforms in policies and practices occurred in 1997, and the following year saw the establishment of a computerized database as a means of reporting adverse events as part of the FDA's post-marketing safety program. Also in 1998, the Pediatric Rule required companies that manufacture drugs and biological products to conduct studies to assess the safety of their products on children.[7]

To protect people of all age groups, the medical community and U.S. government have continued to oversee the development and use of prescription pain relievers and other drugs by establishing new guidelines or adapting old regulations to fit current concerns and needs. If someone were to study a street drug today to see if any legitimate medicinal value could be found, the FDA would still be in charge of regulating that investigation. If, however, a prescription pain reliever already approved by the FDA became abused on the streets or misused without a prescription, the problem and jurisdiction would then fall into the hands of the Drug Enforcement Administration (DEA), whose responsibilities require them to enforce the Controlled Substances Act in overseeing the manufacture, distribution, and dispensing of legally produced and legally controlled drugs.

REWRITING PRESCRIPTIONS FOR PAIN

Just because a prescription pain reliever has been approved by the FDA, legally manufactured, and prescribed by a licensed physician does not guarantee that everyone who takes it will benefit equally. Some patients will not notice any difference in their level of pain, while others may have an allergic reaction or strong side effect leading to an adverse event. Since some side effects can increase over time, it may take a while for adverse reports to come in. In this way the FDA gradually gets more and more patient feedback on each new drug. The drugs have been previously tested, of course, but not on the vast number of people who will use the medication after it receives FDA approval. So information can continue to arrive long after a product has been approved for sale.

On older drugs, investigations may have begun only recently, with new data still being obtained and recorded. Changing times also can change the use or misuse of a drug in a way no one could have foreseen. For example, the opioid drug **propoxyphene** has been around since 1957 and sold under such well-known brand names as Darvon and Darvocet. For more than 50 years doctors prescribed the drug to treat mild to moderate pain with only minimal side effects such as light-headedness, dizziness, and vomiting. So why did the FDA suddenly take action in July 2009 on Darvon and other pain medicines that contain propoxyphene? Reportedly the European medical community saw evidence that this particular opioid might be more deadly than other prescription pain relievers when a patient overlooks or ignores instructions and takes too much. To find out more about this problem, the FDA swiftly set new U.S. studies into motion. While waiting for those results, the FDA believes the benefits of proven pain relief outweigh the safety risks but requires manufacturers of products containing propoxyphene to strengthen warning labels and include in the boxes strong warnings about the potential for overdose. In addition the FDA also requires manufacturers to provide patients with a medication guide emphasizing the importance of using propoxyphene only as directed.[8]

MEDWATCH

The numerous U.S. government regulatory agencies and the medical community at large continue to develop new policies, plans, procedures, laws, regulations, and various means of enforcing all of the above. However, U.S. consumers are the ones who actually use the drugs that have been standardized, monitored, and prescribed. With the advent of the Internet, consumer reporting and government tracking of a drug can now be done fairly easily. Either consumers can ask their doctors to report a problem with a drug to the FDA, or they can fill out a form themselves on a Web site called Med-Watch. By using the Internet to gather reports, the FDA finds out about a problem such as suspected product tampering or poor packaging that can ruin the potency of a drug. More important, the people who use a medication as instructed have an immediate means of reporting serious adverse events such as permanent damage to their health or a severe **drug reaction** requiring emergency hospital treatment.[9]

GETTING A DOCTOR TO PRESCRIBE

Advances in medicine provide more and more choices for people who need prescription pain relievers to treat a medical condition. At the same time governmental controls and media campaigns have also advanced. In the 1980s, for example, First Lady Nancy Reagan popularized the "Just Say No" effort in the U.S. "War Against Drugs." In 2005 the National Youth Antidrug Media Campaign began advertisements and online efforts to encourage teens 14 to 16 to live "Above the Influence." These media campaigns and, especially, open discussions at home and at school have helped teenagers become more aware of the effects of smoking pot and the dangerous risks of using street drugs. Indeed, numerous sources report that marijuana use has declined while the misuse and abuse of prescription pain relievers has markedly risen. Ironically this odd turn of events may also be related to advertising, since teens may assume an advertised product must be safe or it would not be advertised or prescribed by a doctor. No medication, however, is safe when misused or abused. FDA approval, television advertising, and doctor prescriptions merely assure patients that they can use a particular drug in a particular way for a particular reason, trusting that drug to be and do what it says.

In October 1962 the Kefauver-Harris amendments gave the FDA the power to regulate advertisements of prescription drugs to stop false claims about the medicinal effects and contents of a product. In August 1999 the FDA published guidelines for print and broadcast ads requiring drug companies to ensure that their claims:

- are not false or misleading in any respect (For a prescription drug, this would include communicating that the advertised product is available only by prescription and that only a prescribing health care professional can decide whether the product is appropriate for a patient.)
- present a fair balance between information about effectiveness and information about risk
- include a thorough major statement conveying all of the product's most important risk information in consumer-friendly language
- communicate all information relevant to the product's indication (including limitations to use) in consumer-friendly language[10]

Those FDA guidelines started an avalanche of advertising that television viewers and magazine readers see frequently today. In the first year that the FDA guidelines for direct-to-consumer ads took effect, for example, pharmaceutical sales increased $4.20 for every dollar spent on advertising. By 2007 drug companies were spending $4.8 billion per year for direct ads to the public, and by 2008 sales of prescription drugs in the United States had become a $291 billion business. With the exception of New Zealand, advertising prescription drugs directly to the public is legal only in the United States.[11]

3

Chemistry of Prescription Pain Relievers

Terrill and Shona headed down the street toward Bryan's house. Their families had lived in the same neighborhood for years, so neither Terrill's parents nor Shona's foster mom had questioned their plans for the evening. No one seemed to notice the prescription pain relievers missing from the medicine cabinets at home, and if Terrill's grandfather had suspected anything, he did not say a word.

Checking to be sure he still had the small stash of pain meds in his pocket, Terrill asked Shona, "What did you bring?"

*She laughed. "What difference does it make? Everything gets tossed into the **trail mix** anyway. Who knows what we'll get? That's part of the fun though, isn't it?"*

"Yeah," Terrill said, but he felt uneasy. The thought of throwing a bunch of unknown chemicals into his body did not sound like fun. He wanted to see what it felt like to get high, but he had no idea how that happened. He wished he knew more about chemistry and his own body, but until now it had not occurred to him to find out.

Terrill had never been to a pharming party before, but Shona bragged about going—a lot. She told some scary-sounding stories, too, but she seemed to think they were funny—like being run out of an empty warehouse with kids Terrill did not know. Lately, though, she had started making fun of him about being chicken. One time she got mad and said he was boring and had a boring, boring life. Another time she got all weepy and accused him of being too good to hang out with her friends.

For a while Terrill didn't let anything Shona say bother him much, especially since everyone in their neighborhood knew what a hard time she'd had after her parents took off. He put up with her teasing, too, until she started embarrassing him in front of other kids at school. So when Bryan said his parents would be gone for the weekend, Terrill decided that being at a neighbor's house would be better than hanging out in a dilapidated old building in some strange part of town. Now he wasn't sure. He wished he could turn around and go home, but if he did, he knew Shona would never let him hear the end of it. She'd been acting so weird lately, Terrill didn't know what she might do.

OPIOIDS

Inside the pod of each poppy plant lives a variety of **alkaloids**. These natural compounds, which include nitrogen, can be found in all plants and vegetables. As base chemicals, alkaloids react with acids to form salts. Sometimes those salts can be used for medicinal purposes such as pain relief, but this depends on the chemical makeup of the alkaloid.

Most alkaloids have little or no effect on the central nervous system (CNS), so the FDA does not normally regulate those compounds. However, the potent alkaloids in poppy pods, such as the extracts that produce morphine, codeine, and thebaine, are closely regulated by the FDA and governments around the world.

Morphine and codeine act on the CNS to relax the body, but thebaine, which also comes from poppy pods, can be altered for use as a stimulant. Thebaine alkaloids then help to ease symptoms when a patient withdraws from addiction to oxycodone or other narcotics derived from the same poppy plant.

Opioids connect with specific opioid receptors in the brain, spinal cord, and gastrointestinal tract. These drugs have a potent chemical effect on the body as they hold down the activity of nerve cells known to transmit signals of pain. That may sound good, but pain can be a useful tool; for example, in knowing when to step away from a hot surface or when to check for bleeding from a broken glass stab in the foot.

Opioids lessen discomfort mainly by changing the way a person perceives pain. By tapping into the brain's communication system, opioids keep nerve

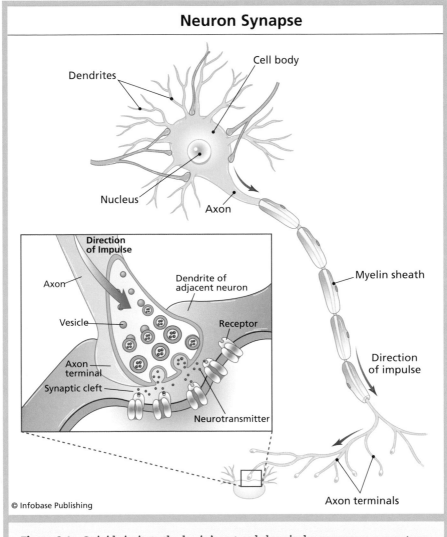

Neuron Synapse

Dendrites

Cell body

Nucleus

Axon

Direction of Impulse

Axon

Dendrite of adjacent neuron

Vesicle

Receptor

Axon terminal

Synaptic cleft

Neurotransmitter

Myelin sheath

Direction of impulse

Axon terminals

© Infobase Publishing

Figure 3.1 Opioids imitate the brain's natural chemical messengers, neurotranmitters, and overstimulate the "reward circuit" of the brain.

cells in the body from doing their usual job of sending, receiving, and processing information. How? According to the article "Understanding Drug Abuse and Addiction" published by the National Institute on Drug Abuse (NIDA), this hindrance happens in two ways: "(1) by imitating the brain's natural chemical messengers, and/or (2) by overstimulating the 'reward circuit' of the brain."

As the NIDA article explained, most drugs flood the brain's reward system with **dopamine**, a **neurotransmitter** in the area of the brain that controls movement, emotion, motivation, and sensations of pleasure. Normally this system aids such survival instincts as sleeping and eating, but overstimulation by an opioid interferes with that vital job, causing such a strong sense of pleasure that the person wants to repeat whatever caused those feelings. This pattern continues until the brain catches on and adapts. Then instead of producing more dopamine, the brain produces less. If the person attempts to regain that first high, more changes in the brain occur, causing potentially permanent damage. As the NIDA article also stated, images of the brains of drug-addicted people show changes that affect judgment, decision making, learning, memory, and control of behavior.

An article on the NIDA for Teens Web site explained how narcotics affect three areas of the brain: (1) the **brain stem**, which controls body functions needed to stay alive, such as breathing, circulating blood, and digesting food; (2) the **limbic system**, which links brain mechanisms that control emotional sensations or responses; and (3) the **cerebral cortex**, or gray matter that makes up about three-fourths of the brain. Divided into four **lobes**, those areas control specific functions, such as processing information from the senses that enable a person to see, feel, hear, and taste. The front part of the cortex, also known as the **forebrain**, functions as the body's "thinking center."

This highly complex communication center works well because of 100 billion neurons that send chemical messages back and forth. As these neurotransmitters travel across the space or **synapse** between neurons, they bind to receptors in a lock-and-key fit for nerve cells. Nevertheless, the NIDA for Teens article warns that some drugs activate neurons since their chemical structure mimics natural neurotransmitters, thereby fooling receptors into activating nerve cells. Unfortunately, the artificial activators do not work exactly the same as a natural neurotransmitter, so the brain sends abnormal messages to the body.[1]

In testimony before the U.S. House of Representatives on prescription **drug abuse**, NIDA director Dr. Nora Volkow expressed concern for adolescents because of the risky trend toward experimenting with drugs while the brain is still developing. Drug exposure interferes with normal development. This is especially true of the prefrontal cortex, which controls judgment and decision making and is the last area of the brain to mature. This developmental sequence also explains why some teenagers seem especially prone to take ill-advised risks such as abusing or experimenting with drugs.

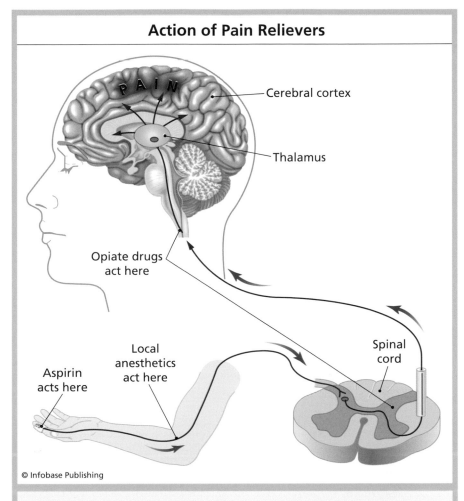

Action of Pain Relievers

PAIN

Cerebral cortex

Thalamus

Opiate drugs
act here

Local
anesthetics
act here

Aspirin
acts here

Spinal
cord

© Infobase Publishing

Figure 3.2 Different types of painkillers act on different areas of the nervous system. Aspirin acts by reducing pain signals in the distant peripheral nerves, such as those in the finger. Local anesthetics block pain signals traveling up the nerve, while opioids manage pain processing in the brain and spinal cord.

NONSTEROIDAL ANTI-INFLAMMATORY DRUGS

Nonsteroidal anti-inflammatory drugs (NSAIDs) such as aspirin, ibuprofen, and naproxen interact with the body by hindering a **protein enzyme** called **cyclooxygenase**, or COX, from doing its job. One form of the enzyme, COX-1, maintains kidney function and protects the lining of the stomach from being injured by digestive acids. The other form, COX-2, produces heat

HOW OPIOIDS AFFECT THE BODY

Drugs have a chemical effect on the natural chemistry of the body, bringing positive or negative impact and often a bit of both. Depending on the strength and dosage, opioids affect the major systems of the body in the following ways:

Effects on the Central Nervous System

- Pain relief as the person's perception of pain begins to change
- Drowsiness or sedation with high doses potentially producing convulsions
- Euphoria or sense of well-being regardless of actual circumstances
- Mental confusion causing what's real to appear unreal or vice versa
- Respiratory depression with large doses often causing respiratory failure
- Queasiness, nausea, vomiting
- Suppression of the cough reflex
- Dilated pupils or pinpoint pupils indicating morphine overdose

Effects on the Gastrointestinal Tract

- Constipation
- Intestinal spasms

Effects on the Heart

- **Bradycardia**, or slow heartbeat, with very high doses

Effects on the Urinary Tract

- Urinary retention[2]

or inflammation around an injured joint to warm the area, increase circulation, and assist healing. By blocking COX actions NSAIDs ease pain, fever, and inflammation, but they also block the body's natural protection of the kidneys and stomach. For this reason, NSAIDs can upset the stomach and cause internal bleeding.

About 20 drugs fall into the NSAID category, but not acetaminophen (Tylenol) since it does not reduce inflammation. In addition acetaminophen does not act on the stomach as NSAIDs do but on the liver, making excessive dosages extremely **toxic**. Two of the most popular PPRs in the world, Percocet and Vicodin, are opioid analgesics that contain acetaminophen. Because of this a federal advisory panel recommended that the FDA place a ban on Percocet and Vicodin. The panel also mentioned tolerance occurring with both drugs, which means that patients taking them for long periods of time need more or higher dosages to get the level of pain relief they first had. The advisory committee did not single out those two drugs, however. It also recommended a ban on other prescription drugs that include acetaminophen because of the potential for liver damage with increased usage or doses. In addition the federal advisory panel recommended that the FDA reduce the amount of acetaminophen allowed in combination drugs, so the highest amount would drop from 500 milligrams to 325.[3]

HOW LONG DO DRUGS STAY IN THE SYSTEM?

The amount of time a drug stays in the body depends on such personal factors as:

- age
- weight and body fat
- general health
- regularity of exercise
- intensity of physical activities
- state of mind
- frequency of drug use

The potency of a narcotic also affects how long a drug stays in a person's system. Generally some evidence of opiates will remain in the body for one to two days and methadone up to a week. If, however, the person has been using drugs often or for a long period of time, a cumulative effect can occur, making a drug detectable for many days beyond the norm.[4]

DANGEROUS DRUG INTERACTIONS

The potential for drug abuse depends on the type of prescription pain reliever, the dosage, the amount of time the person has been taking the drug, and the method by which the drug is taken. Swallowing a pill slows the effect on the body simply because the drug takes longer to reach peak plasma concentration in the bloodstream. With a hypodermic needle or nasal spray the user experiences a quick rush, since those methods deliver narcotics speedily to the brain. However, people who get immediate pleasure with the fastest high may also be quicker to become abusers of the drug in their effort to regain that first rush, again and again.

According to the Centers for Disease Control and Prevention (CDC), 40% of all poisoning deaths in the United States in 2006 involved opioid pain relievers—a 20% increase since 1999. The CDC further reported that the greatest increase came from the long-lasting opioid methadone, commonly used to treat symptoms of withdrawal from drug addiction. The number of deaths from drug poisoning involving methadone dramatically increased from 790 in 1999 to 5,420 in 2006. Methadone patients who also took antianxiety medications comprised 17% of the deaths attributed to drug poisoning. However, 50% of the deaths involving opioids combined that narcotic with at least one other type of drug.[5]

Although those drugs may be other prescription medications, over-the-counter products can also interact with each other, causing toxicity or dangerous side effects not usually associated with the drugs. For example, the combination of an opioid with a sleep drug and/or an OTC **antihistamine** commonly used to combat allergies would be likely to cause a dangerous incident of oversedation, since each of those products induces sleep. Alcohol, which is also a drug, encourages drowsiness too. Therefore, combining opioids with sleeping pills, antihistamines, and alcohol—whether from an OTC cough medicine or wine, beer, and other alcoholic beverages—is a perilous practice that can be fatal.

WHEN DO DRUGS EXPIRE?

The testing data from the drug Shelf Life Extension Program (SLEP) that the FDA provided the U.S. Army has officially been declared "For Official Use

DRUG SAFETY FOR KIDS AND TEENS

According to the FDA, a child is a person 17 years old or younger, but here's the problem: Only 50% to 60% of prescription drugs have been tested on children or teens. Prescription medication information sheets include a pediatric section that indicates whether a drug has been child-tested, but few over-the-counter (OTC) products have been studied to determine the proper dosage or effectiveness and safety in children. Indeed, with the exception of medicines commonly used to treat fever or pain, OTC products have not been tested in children at all. For products intended only for children, children *must* be tested. Despite this regulation, the combined percentage of OTC products and prescription pain relievers that have been tested on infants currently remains at about zero.[6]

Only." According to information on the U.S. Army Medical Materiel Agency Web site, non-SLEP organizations that use SLEP information violate the federal law governing misbranded pharmaceuticals.[7]

Why is information about the ultimate expiration date of drugs being kept secret? As the FDA explained, expiration dating might underestimate the actual shelf life of a drug, causing people to use medications that has become unstable, ineffective, or otherwise unsafe. Also, patients themselves do not normally stockpile drugs in unopened containers as the U.S. Army must do in order to keep adequate supplies on hand. When medical supplies for the military began to get close to the expiration dates on the label, the military needed to find out if they had to throw those drugs away. It conducted tests that showed that most medications can still be used past the expiration date, but because of the high variability, drugs would have to be tested and evaluated by lot to assure stability and quality of the product.[8] This is the bottom line: If the label on an open container says a drug has expired, believe it!

4

Prescription for Addiction

At the end of a cul-de-sac and surrounded by trees, Mike's house almost seemed to disappear into the sound-muffling woods. Spacious yards between the nice homes meant the neighbors wouldn't be likely to complain about the noise when Bryan's parents returned home from their long weekend.

As Joe and Katie reached the front door, Joe hesitated, trying to decide whether to go in or go home. As he stepped into the living room, he could see Katie rushing like a crazy person toward Mike, who held out an open bag. Katie shoved one hand into the brown paper sack then drew out a fistful of something that she quickly popped into her mouth and downed with a can of beer.

"Is that your girlfriend?" someone asked, and Joe gave a little jump. He hadn't even noticed Hannah, sitting alone in the foyer.

"Just a neighbor," Joe answered, wondering if his cheeks had turned as red as they felt. He often looked for Hannah at school, but he'd never let her know it. "I'm surprised to see you here," he said now.

"Me too," Hannah said.

Joe was still trying to think of something else to say when Mike's loud laugh distracted him. "Sounds like he's having a good time."

Hannah shrugged. "That's what he says, but he's just not the same Mike I've known since we were kids."

"Really? I hadn't noticed anything different about him," Joe said, but he now noticed Hannah's frown. "Is that why you're here tonight—because Mike's parents aren't?"

Hannah looked embarrassed. "Maybe. I don't know."

"Me either," Joe admitted. Had he come to get high or to keep Katie from pestering him forever? Either way, here he was, sitting in a dark foyer next to Mike's self-appointed babysitter. Now what? he wondered. He could hang out with Hannah, or he could head toward Katie and her prescription pain relievers.

According to Dr. Alan I. Leshner, director of the National Institute of Drug Abuse (NIDA), some young people use drugs just to feel good, but others, who may be suffering emotionally, use drugs to feel better or more like other kids. This latter group often includes teens in difficult situations such as dysfunctional families, poverty, or abuse, but may include young people with various types of mental disorders such as clinical depression, panic disorders, or schizophrenia that have not been properly treated. Dr. Leshner went on to say that about 10 million children and adolescents have emotional and psychiatric problems that compromise their ability to function, placing this group at an extremely high risk for addiction. Medical research shows this type of drug misuse or abuse only worsens the underlying psychological problems.

Of course, not all teens use drugs and not all are even tempted to do so. Dr. Leshner had an encouraging word: "If a child reaches the age of 20 without using alcohol, tobacco or marijuana, the probability is almost zero he or she will ever develop a serious drug problem."[1]

HOW ADDICTION WORKS

According to the National Institutes of Health (NIH), addictive drugs stimulate opiate receptors in the body, causing the person to experience pleasure, euphoria, and feelings of reward in a briefly felt "rush" followed by a few relaxing hours of contentment. However, this reward system can lead to addiction, since the drug changes the way nerve cells work in the brain. After a while the cells get so used to having a narcotic that "they need it to work normally. This, in turn, leads to addiction. If opiates are taken away from dependent nerve cells, these cells become overactive. Eventually, they will work normally again, but in the meantime, they create a range of symptoms known as withdrawal."[2]

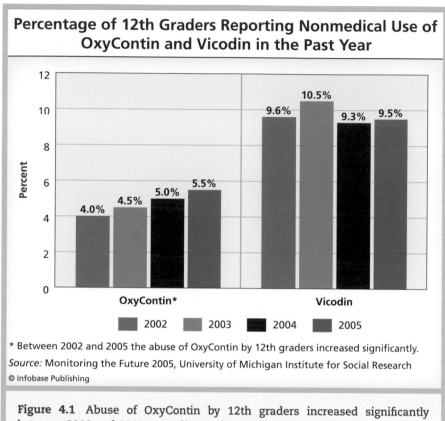

Percentage of 12th Graders Reporting Nonmedical Use of OxyContin and Vicodin in the Past Year

OxyContin*: 4.0% (2002), 4.5% (2003), 5.0% (2004), 5.5% (2005)

Vicodin: 9.6% (2002), 10.5% (2003), 9.3% (2004), 9.5% (2005)

■ 2002   ■ 2003   ■ 2004   ■ 2005

* Between 2002 and 2005 the abuse of OxyContin by 12th graders increased significantly.

Source: Monitoring the Future 2005, University of Michigan Institute for Social Research

© Infobase Publishing

Figure 4.1 Abuse of OxyContin by 12th graders increased significantly between 2002 and 2005, according to the 2005 Monitoring the Future Survey.

Besides this cycle of addiction, according to the *Physicians' Desktop Reference* (PDR), some drugs have reinforcing properties that make them even more likely to become addictive. The method of taking a drug affects this potential too. For instance, smoking or inhaling a narcotic puts the drug into the bloodstream quickly, making it more potent and potentially more addictive than swallowing a pill. However, people with a biological or environmental predisposition for drug abuse can be affected rapidly by a pill or capsule, even if the drug has only low reinforcing properties for addiction.

In discussing additional concerns, the PDR article highlighted the differences between **drug dependence**, tolerance, drug abuse, and addiction. With physical tolerance, for example, patients need a stronger dosage or an additional drug to experience the same quality of pain relief they first felt. On the other hand, a drug-dependent person adapts to a medication she actually needs for a while, but later cannot stop taking it without symptoms of withdrawal. Those unpleasant sensations then cause people to crave relief until they begin to lose control over the times and amounts of the drugs they have taken. Although this can, and often does, lead to drug addiction, a person can also become addicted to a drug that does not produce physical dependence. In each of those situations, drug abusers typically underestimate their drug intake and try to hide their addiction from others and themselves. Even if they are aware of the dangers of street drugs, they might not realize they can, and perhaps already have, become addicted to OTC products or prescription pain relievers.[3]

THOSE AT RISK FOR DRUG ABUSE

Addiction does not happen overnight or with one-time misuse of a drug, yet those who turn to drugs as a means of comforting themselves are at a particularly high risk for drug misuse and abuse. An article titled "Drug Abuse and Addiction" on the Helpguide.org Web site said, "A powerful force in addiction is the inability to self-soothe or get relief from untreated mental or physical pain."[4]

The article also expressed concern over other factors known to put people at higher risk for eventual addiction to drugs:

- Family history of drug use, misuse, and abuse
- Patient history of mental illness
- Pressures from friends who experiment with or abuse drugs
- Physical pain treated without medical supervision

Other factors such as poor social skills, poverty, academic failure, lack of parental supervision, and plain old boredom may also come into play. No single factor can predict what will happen, of course, but combining one or more of these risk factors can increase the probability of addiction to illegal narcotics and also to prescription pain relievers and/or OTC drugs.

The risks for abuse increase when combining such factors as a person's biological makeup, social environment, age, and stage of development. For

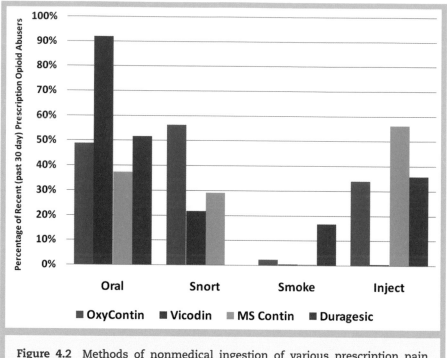

Figure 4.2 Methods of nonmedical ingestion of various prescription pain relivers. (S. H. Budman et al., "Can Abuse Deterrent Formulations Make a Difference? Expectation and Speculation," *Harm Reduction Journal* 6, no. 8 [May 29, 2009]. Used under Creative Commons License.)

example, the genes present at birth can combine with detrimental influences in the home and school environment, increasing a person's vulnerability. The age or developmental stage of the person adds to that risk, mainly because early drug use raises the odds of addiction. Why? According to a Reuters article on OxyContin published in 2008, "The brain undergoes dramatic changes in adolescence . . . and there is evidence that abusing opioids during this key developmental period may cause permanent brain alterations that increase the likelihood that a teen will be more vulnerable to addiction compared with those who first abuse this drug as adults."[5]

In a 2008 issue of *Clinician Reviews* the article "Teen Prescription Drug Abuse: A National Epidemic" said that nonmedical use of drugs varies by regions and cultures, but 12- to 17-year-old girls will be more apt to misuse pain relievers than boys. Outside that age group, however, males are more likely to abuse prescription drugs. The article also reported that the prevalence of teen drug abuse among American Indians and Alaska Natives stood at 17% whereas the lowest rate, 7%, occurred among youth of Asian descent.

Regardless of race or gender, the highest rate of drug abuse among adolescents reportedly occurs in small cities and states in the West, while urban areas in the Northeast have the lowest incidents of drug problems. The article indicated that having strong religious beliefs and positive interactions with parents and other family members will lower the likelihood of drug misuse, abuse, and addiction.

On the other hand, the method by which a person chooses to take drugs will often increase the risk of addiction. For example, injecting or inhaling drugs gives an immediate high that users then want to repeat. Many teens and young adults feel repulsed by the idea of a needle and do not want to risk contracting HIV or other blood-borne diseases. However, if they spend time with drug abusers who inject themselves, they may eventually get used to the idea or get over their squeamishness. Some teens also think that injecting a drug usually means they do not need as many narcotics or as strong a dosage to get high.

An article in the May 2009 issue of *Harm Reduction Journal* said that the longer people abuse an opioid, the more likely they will be to try an alternate route such as injecting or snorting drugs, rather than swallowing. The means of administering a narcotic also indicates the likelihood of abusing illegal drugs and acquiring severe problems in functioning as a young adult. Therefore, the younger the abuser, the higher the likelihood of adverse risks and reactions as the teen matures.

Based on research findings by Trevor Bennett, an article for the Center for Problem-Oriented Policing took a different approach in discussing steps that may or may not lead to addiction. After reviewing current literature on drugs and interviewing opioid users, Bennett found that addiction begins with the decision to try a drug, for example out of curiosity or because of the influence of friends. It then usually takes more than a year before the person becomes addicted, but that does not necessarily mean a loss of control. According to Bennett's findings, addicts often stop taking drugs for days, weeks, or even years. Therefore, he suggested looking deeper into elements of rationality and choice in the development of addiction. He also challenged earlier theories that stress the compulsiveness of drug use, saying they offer only a limited view of the overall opioid picture. For instance, theories regarding compulsion of drug use do not account for the variations that occur with drug choices, nor do they explain why some people who are predisposed to addiction never take drugs and others who become addicted might have long periods of abstinence. He suggested that a broader theory of drug use and addiction would need to consider individual perceptions and decision making. The author also suggested a general change of perspective in how addicts are viewed. For instance, instead of seeing addicts as having a physical and/ or mental condition requiring medical treatment, Bennett suggested a shift in thinking toward the greater use of police and the court system as a means of dealing with addiction.[6]

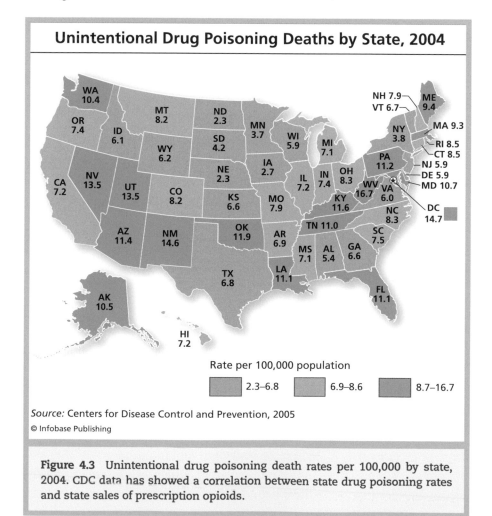

Unintentional Drug Poisoning Deaths by State, 2004

Rate per 100,000 population

2.3–6.8   6.9–8.6   8.7–16.7

Source: Centers for Disease Control and Prevention, 2005

© Infobase Publishing

Figure 4.3 Unintentional drug poisoning death rates per 100,000 by state, 2004. CDC data has showed a correlation between state drug poisoning rates and state sales of prescription opioids.

> ## SIGNS OF ADDICTION
>
> - Sleep problems—too much or too little
> - Sudden changes in weight
> - Changes in clothing choices such as the use of long sleeves, long pants, and socks to hide needle tracks
> - Deterioration of health—for instance, a chronic cough or sinus problems which may or may not include nosebleed
> - Deterioration of teeth
> - Odd or argumentative behavior
> - Extreme reactions or paranoia about privacy; for example, as the person attempts to hide drugs, excessive amounts of cash, or drug paraphernalia such as a pipe or hypodermic needle

EFFECTS OF DRUGS

Being compelled by drugs to use drugs causes a disruptive cycle that affects pretty much everything in or around a person's life. With heavy misuse and addiction many people become increasingly powerless as their drug of choice carries more and more clout, command, and control. The drug makes the decisions with no regard for how this might affect the person's health, relationships, education, and future.

According to an article on PPR abuse published in a 2009 issue of the *Journal of the American Academy of Child and Adolescent Psychiatry,* 52% of 12- to 17-year-old adolescents with a history of using nonprescribed PPRs had tried hydrocodone products; 50% had used propoxyphene (Darvocet or Darvon) or codeine (such as Tylenol with codeine), and 24% had tried oxycodone products such as Percocet or OxyContin, all of which have a potent effect. The article said the average age for beginning nonprescribed PPR use is 13.3 years, compared to 13.1 for first use of alcohol and 13.6 for marijuana usage. Compared to nonusers, adolescents who try nonprescribed PPRs increase their odds of using alcohol and other drugs, becoming involved in criminal activities, receiving emergency treatment, and needing services for mental and physical health problems.[7]

What started as an individual choice and private concern eventually affects more people than a single drug abuser might imagine. As the situation of that one person multiplies by millions, the entire country can feel and reel under a heavy burden. Families disintegrate. Workers lose jobs. Learners fail to learn. Children become abused. Domestic and public acts of violence increase. Property gets stolen to pay for drugs or destroyed during bouts of the erratic behavior caused by drug abuse.

As reported in an article published in the *Harm Reduction Journal,* nonprescribed use of drugs and nonconventional ways of administering them seem to be associated with poor relationships, poor work performance, legal problems, and increased incidents of violence, homelessness, overdose, and death.

In addition to the human costs, the astonishing economic costs of drug abuse may help to show the magnitude of impact that each person's drug misuse has on countless others. For example, the report "NIDA InfoFacts: Understanding Drug Abuse and Addiction," cited earlier, estimated that losses in productivity and increases in expenditures for health care and criminal justice make the overall cost of substance abuse in the United States exceed half a trillion dollars a year.

5
Treatment and Recovery

Matt and Jim hung out in the foyer at Kim's house, talking while a party went on around them. Suddenly someone shouted, "Jill's down! Call 911!"

Before Matt could reach for the cell phone he usually kept in his pocket, Jim had placed the call and given Kim's street address with directions to the house. He stayed on the line answering questions as Matt rushed into the living room where a half-dozen or so kids hovered around Jill, who lay motionless on the floor.

"Hey! Move back! Give her some space," Matt ordered. He tried to remember anything else useful he had seen on TV. Breathing. See if she's breathing, he reminded himself. When he couldn't tell, he felt panicked but still managed to grab Jill's wrist to check for a pulse. Wow, that's slow! he thought, but at least she's alive.

Matt sat back on his heels, relieved he did not have to perform mouth-to-mouth resuscitation before the paramedics arrived. Jill looked really sweet lying there so still and pale, but she smelled strongly of beer and vomit.

"Does anybody know how much she had to drink or what pills she took?" Matt asked. He felt certain the paramedics would need to know that information right away to give Jill whatever treatment she needed, but no one answered, and the whole room got unusually quiet. Looking around, Matt saw only Jim and Kim standing over him. "Where did everybody go?" he asked.

"Where do you think," Kim said. "Man, this party's over!"

HOW DOES AN OVERDOSE HAPPEN?

Whether accidental or intentional, a drug overdose occurs when a person takes a higher dosage of a medication than the physician prescribed. Sensitivity to a PPR can cause a toxic reaction, too, increasing the risk of side effects that overwhelm the body. Most often these life-threatening incidents happen among preschool children and among people ranging in age from teens to adults in their mid-30s.[1]

The causes of accidental overdose usually differ according to the age group. For example, a curious toddler might put a small item into the mouth as a means of exploring new information through the senses of taste and touch. The sound of a shaken pill bottle can be enticing, too, since the noise sounds similar to rattling toys made for babies and toddlers, causing young children to think they have found a new plaything. If the cap comes off easily, any non-childproof container left within a young child's reach can become especially hazardous. To avoid such dangers all prescription medications and over-the-counter drugs need to be kept securely, locked up or out of reach, to protect young children and crawling infants from drug poisoning or accidental overdose.

If a household includes known drug abusers, teenagers with mental health problems, or anyone of any age who seems inclined toward suicidal thoughts, confusion, or self-harming behavior, medications should be placed out of sight and/or stored in a locked cabinet. For a variety of reasons (as discussed in this book), some people misuse prescription pain relievers intentionally. Although this does not always mean the person meant to overdose, the end result can be the same or worse. For instance, if no one knows what drug the person has taken or how much, an overdose will be more likely to result in death before the appropriate medical treatment can be given.

DRUG OVERDOSE

Acetaminophen

People often think of a drug overdose as the result of buying bad drugs on the street, miscalculating the dosage of a prescription pain reliever, or regularly abusing or misusing a drug until an overdose inevitably happens. However, acetaminophen poisoning—a toxic overdose—occurs frequently because of the popularity and high availability of that substance in OTC drugs and medications prescribed for cold, flu, cough, and pain. According to the Merck Manuals Online Medical Library, more than 100 OTC products contain acetaminophen and so do some PPRs such as Tylenol 3 with codeine. Since acetaminophen acts on the liver instead of the stomach (as aspirin and other NSAIDs do), permanent liver damage and even death can occur unless the patient receives prompt medical treatment.

The signs of an acetaminophen overdose commonly include nausea and vomiting in the first 24 hours, severe abdominal pain within 24 to 72 hours, the typically skin-yellowing signs of liver failure in 3 to 4 days and, in 5 days, general organ failure and death. To reverse those potential effects of poisoning and avert permanent damage to the liver and other organs, patients who receive emergency treatment for acetaminophen overdose may be given the **antidote** N-acetyl cysteine.[2]

Aspirin

Prescription strength aspirin can also contain the mild opioid codeine, which adds to the signs of an overdose as discussed in the entry below. On its own, however, too much aspirin can cause dizziness, rapid heartbeat, and hyperactivity or drowsiness and fatigue. Ringing in the ears and even temporary deafness can occur, and massive overdoses can produce high fever, seizures, and coma.

In extreme cases of aspirin poisoning, the MedlinePlus Web site says that **hemodialysis** may be needed to remove poisonous toxins from the bloodstream. It also reported that more than 150 milligrams of aspirin per kilogram of body weight can cause serious, even fatal, results if the patient does not receive rapid medical treatment. For a teenager or small-sized adult, that dosage equals about 20 tablets of 325 mg aspirin, but children can be severely affected by much smaller amounts.[3]

Codeine and Other Opioids

Often combined with acetaminophen and aspirin in prescription pain medications, the mild opioid codeine can show its own signs of overdose in pinpoint pupils and seizures typical of an opioid overdose. According to MedlinePlus, toxic amounts of codeine can also be suspected if a patient has breathing difficulties, extreme drowsiness, and a dangerous drop in blood pressure (BP).

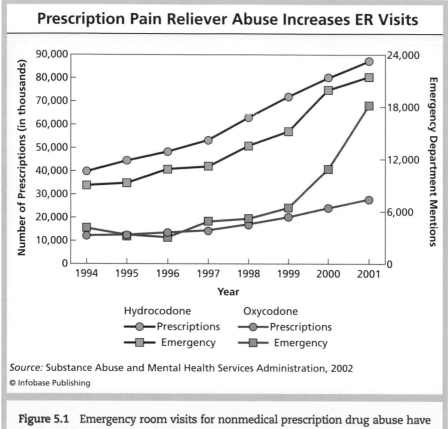

Figure 5.1 Emergency room visits for nonmedical prescription drug abuse have increased in recent years alongside increases in pain reliever prescriptions.

If no BP monitor can be found nearby or if there is no time to use it, cold clammy skin can indicate excessively low blood pressure or a dramatic drop in BP. By comparison and also contrast, an overdose of cocaine will be likely to cause both the blood pressure and heart rate to rise to a dangerously high level, potentially causing a stroke or seizure.

Characteristically, opioids depress the central nervous system. Therefore, an overdose of this narcotic even in weaker forms will be more likely to lower the heart rate, weaken the pulse rate, and decrease the rate of breathing. As occurs with even the milder codeine, an opioid overdose can cause dizziness, faintness, vomiting, slowed heart rate, trouble breathing, and sometimes convulsions. If the narcotic has been inhaled or injected directly into a vein or if a stronger form of the drug has been used, an opioid over-dose can lead to cardiac arrest, potentially causing the patient to go into a coma or die.

COMMON SIGNS OF OPIOID OVERDOSE

The signs of a drug overdose vary according to the type, strength, and amount of the prescription pain reliever involved. Regardless of which PPR was taken, however, these common signs show the need for prompt medical attention.

- Difficulty walking
- Difficulty talking or making sense
- Difficulty breathing
- Vomiting or nausea
- Sweating and fever or very dry, hot skin
- Hyperactivity or strong signs of agitation
- Aggressive, violent, or unusually hostile behavior
- Delusions or hallucinations
- Body tremors, shakes, or convulsions
- Excessive drowsiness
- Extremely small ("pinpoint") pupils
- Pupils that do not react to light
- Unconsciousness, coma, or death

FIRST AID

First aid should start with safety precautions by the person who tries to help. The National Institutes of Health (NIH) warns that people should not risk their own well-being by trying to subdue someone who is behaving erratically or having a violent outburst after taking too many drugs. Trying to reason with that person or offer advice of any kind will not be effective and can cause the irrational behavior to become even more unpredictable and potentially threatening.

Whenever a drug overdose is suspected, first aid should rapidly begin with a local 911 call to ask for an ambulance and emergency medical response team. Depending on the situation and type of substance involved, the National

Poison Control Center can be reached from any location in the United States by calling (800) 222-1222.

   After someone has placed a call for emergency medical assistance, the following first aid measures suggested by the NIH will usually benefit a patient until professional help can arrive. These suggestions only bring temporary relief, however, and are not meant to be used either as medical advice or as the main source of medical treatment.

1. If the patient seems to be conscious and breathing, speak calmly. Offer reassurance that help is on the way. Unless the person seems hostile or menacing, try to prevent the patient from taking more drugs. If possible, find out which drugs were taken, how many, and when. That information can help medical personnel to save a life.

2. Do not try to get the patient to vomit unless the Poison Control Center specifically says so. If vomiting happens on its own, turn the person's head to the side to lessen the risk of choking. Do not give the patient anything to eat or drink.

3. Look for signs of shock such as decreased alertness, cold, clammy skin, and a blue tinge to the fingernails or lips. If the person has none of those symptoms but seems very sleepy, try to keep the patient awake. Walk the person around. If, however, signs of shock do exist, ease the patient into a flat reclining position, then slightly elevate the feet. Loosen any belt, scarf, tie, or other clothing that restricts breathing. Keep the person warm.

4. If the patient becomes unconscious, check vital signs often to make sure that breathing has not stopped. Do not leave the patient's side. Do not slap the person or pour water on the face or attempt any other type of "wake-up call," because they will not work: the patient is not sleeping, but unconscious. Do, however, add additional covers if needed for warmth.

5. Check the pulse rate and **respiration** (breathing rate) every few minutes until medical help arrives. Most teenagers and adults take about 12 to 20 breaths per minute, but that can vary from person to person. If the fingernails have turned purplish or blue and the breathing seems labored, this may indicate that the patient does not have enough oxygen going into the lungs and bloodstream.

6. If the patient stops breathing, check the mouth and throat for obstacles. Clear any obstruction to breathing. If possible, find someone with CPR (**cardiopulmonary resuscitation**) training to perform that life-saving procedure immediately to keep the heart beating.

7. If a seizure begins, do not try to move the patient, but do clear the surrounding area of any sharp items and also large or hard objects that might cause harm. Do not restrain the person. Do not put anything into the person's mouth, but do put a cushion beneath the head to lessen bumps and bruising.

8. Once consciousness has been regained, test for mental alertness by asking a simple question such as "What's your name?" or "How old are you?"

9. As soon as possible, inquire about the symptoms. For instance, find out if the person has dizziness, a bad headache, or any chest pain. Ask for a specific location and description of the discomfort or of anything abnormal that the patient is experiencing.

10. After professional help has arrived, look around for any drug containers that the person may have used, and take those to the hospital. If no one knows what drugs were taken, but the person threw up, use a small zip-top freezer bag to transport the vomit to the hospital laboratory. Gross though this may be, the contents can provide the very information needed to begin life-saving treatment before it's too late.[4]

EMERGENCY MEDICAL RESCUE IN DRUG OVERDOSE

As soon as emergency care has arrived, the medical team will need to know exactly what symptoms the person has experienced and also the type, amount, and method of the drug or drugs taken. Patient information such as age, approximate weight, and any known allergies or medical conditions can be crucial too.

Just as the signs of an overdose will vary according to the amount and chemical makeup of a drug, the life-saving treatments performed by the medical team might also be different from one person to the next. Generally speaking though, emergency medical treatment will begin by stabilizing the patient's vital signs (heart rate, pulse rate, and breathing), then removing toxins from the bloodstream before those poisons can permanently damage or completely shut down a **vital organ** (heart, lungs, liver, kidneys) of the body.

The amount of time that has passed from when the person took too many drugs to when medical help arrived will also affect the emergency treatment. If help arrived very quickly, the treatment might include pumping the stomach, assuming the patient did not inject or snort a drug but swallowed too many pills. Stomach pumping involves putting a tube into the patient's mouth and down the throat into the stomach to empty the contents safely. If vomiting has already occurred, this may not be needed. Otherwise, heaving up a poison without that tube can cause further tissue damage in the stomach, esophagus, and other soft tissue along the way. Since a medically inserted tube provides a much safer means of emptying the contents of the stomach, inducing nausea or getting a drug abuser to throw up on purpose is almost never recommended.

In the hospital or emergency care clinic, the patient's pulse rate, breathing rate, body temperature, and blood pressure will continue to be monitored. To cleanse the toxins from the body and bloodstream, the patient will be likely to receive the following:

- activated charcoal to help neutralize drug poisoning
- artificial respiration or oxygen to assist breathing
- intravenous (IV) medication injected into a vein to administer life-saving treatment quickly
- **intravenous fluids** to keep the body hydrated with the water and minerals that are vital to life.

Multiple doses of medication may be needed, too, to reverse the toxic effects of the drug. If that drug happens to be a heavy dose of acetaminophen, the patient will also be given N-acetyl cysteine to counteract poisons in the liver.

To treat an opioid overdose, the standard hospital procedure is to provide a medication such as **naloxone** to counteract the effects of respiratory depression so the patient can begin to breathe normally. A drug such as **buprenorphine** might be added too, or used alone to treat drug cravings, mainly because counteracting medications can cause side effects similar to a "cold turkey" type of drug withdrawal. Sometimes, though, the medical team may give a general anesthesia to avoid the pain of abrupt withdrawal in a patient who needs to **detoxify** quickly.

WITHDRAWAL SYMPTOMS

Symptoms vary according to the type of narcotic and the length of time the person has abused that drug. For example, a person withdrawing from an addiction to an over-the-counter (OTC) product might not experience the severity of symptoms associated with withdrawal from opioids and other drugs. Nevertheless, symptoms commonly include:

- shakes and tremor
- chills or sweating
- severe muscle pain or cramping
- insomnia and restlessness
- extreme anxiety and generally jittery feelings
- irritability
- panic attacks
- depression

Besides those general symptoms of withdrawal, opioid addicts who withdraw from drug use might also experience:

- runny eyes and nose
- nausea, vomiting, and diarrhea
- stomach cramps
- rapid heartbeat or arrhythmia
- high blood pressure
- hallucinations
- psychotic behavior

The very title of an article in *Medical News Today* warned that "Abrupt Opioid Withdrawal Increases Pain Sensitivity." The article explained that painful stimuli in the spinal cord can trigger a long-lasting "pain memory" when a person goes off an opioid too quickly. On the other hand, slow withdrawal can keep that person from becoming more sensitive than normal to pain. In

TYPES OF DRUG TREATMENT PROGRAMS

The Centers for Disease Control and Prevention (CDC) listed the following types of treatment used to help addicts get off and stay off drugs.[5]

- **Detoxification (Detox) Program**—provides short-term medical supervision as a patient withdraws from drug use or abuse.
- **Residential Treatment**—brings recovering addicts together in medically supervised housing where individual and group therapy sessions regularly occur.
- **Therapeutic Community**—helps recovering addicts living in a group residence setting usually for about 6 to 18 months to learn more effective and beneficial ways of coping mentally, physically, medically, socially, and legally.
- **Outpatient Treatment**—provides an option for those who have a stable family life or career to live at home while participating in group counseling sessions, intensive day treatment, drug education programs, and self-help or 12-step groups.
- **Medication-assisted Treatment**—provides patients with medications such as methadone but works best when combined with drug counseling and appropriate behavioral therapy.
- **Support Groups**—do not treat the medical needs involved with substance abuse but do provide emotional and social support as participants develop skills useful to their ongoing recovery and a productive life.
- **12-Step Program**—based on the successful Alcoholics Anonymous (AA) program, helps recovering addicts to encourage one another in abstaining from drugs.

some cases, a patient may also be prescribed a calcium channel blocker to stop hypersensitivity to pain before it begins.[6]

TREATMENT FOR DRUG ADDICTION

After providing medical treatment to help a drug overdose patient to detoxify as safely and quickly as possible, the health team at a hospital or clinic

Figure 5.2 Methadone is often used to lessen the harsh symptoms of withdrawal during treatment for opioid addiction. (© *Photo Researchers, Inc.*)

will assess the particular needs of that individual. For instance, some patients may have formerly untreated psychiatric problems that led them to overdose intentionally, in which case suicide prevention or a variety of mental health therapies may now become the main focus of care. Other people may have overdosed accidentally but are not addicted to narcotics, so they do not need treatment for drug addiction. Instead they might need a more workable plan for managing chronic pain. Sometimes, however, further investigation will show that a drug overdose occurred because the patient regularly misuses or abuses drugs and needs to be admitted to a facility that specializes in treating drug addiction.

For patients addicted to opioids and opiates, medications such as methadone, buprenorphine, and **naltrexone** (a derivative of naloxone) may be used as part of the treatment program. Those drugs relieve the physical symptoms of withdrawal; while behavioral therapies address the mental, emotional, and social attitudes that may have led to drug addiction in the first place. For example, behavioral therapy helps to keep people motivated in taking an active part in their drug treatment by offering ways to avoid drug use and cope with drug cravings but also by helping patients to deal with a relapse should one occur. In addition, behavioral therapy can help active participants to improve their communication skills, their relationships with friends, and the overall dynamics within their families. Individual therapy sessions will usually be part of the treatment program too. However, group therapy can create a safe, positive environment for individuals to come together to support one another, give each other feedback, and try new or more effective ways of coping and relating to other people at home, work, and school.

As a public health concern, drug abuse affects many more people than just the addict, and so does the successful recovery of each individual. Even if a person does not have health insurance or the money needed for a residential drug withdrawal program, other monies may be available. For instance,

MORE ABOUT METHADONE

This synthetic drug has been used for decades to treat opioid and opiate addictions by occupying opioid receptors in the brain, thus making less room for the opioids themselves. Taken orally each day, methadone quickly goes to work for 24 to 36 hours, keeping drug addicts from experiencing harsh symptoms of withdrawal. Since it is a narcotic itself, methadone must be prescribed and supervised by a doctor. However, the drug does not impair judgment or upset such normal activities as attending school, driving a car, or holding down a job. Mild side effects such as constipation, skin rash, and drowsiness may occur but usually lessen over time or with an adjustment in the dosage.

A fact sheet from the American Association for the Treatment of Opioid Dependence reported that every dollar spent on methadone helps the economy four times as much, mainly by reducing crime. Methadone reduces exposure to the HIV/AIDS virus, too, by reducing cravings for a high, which reduces needle sharing among opioid and opiate addicts. Reportedly, pregnant women can also go onto a doctor-supervised program of methadone with no harm to themselves or the fetus.[7]

the article "Principles of Drug Addiction Treatment" on the National Institute on Drug Abuse (NIDA) Web site pointed out that private and employer-subsidized health plans often cover some type of treatment for drug addiction. Local, state, and federal government funds may also be available, although the funding might go up or down depending on the overall health and stability of the national economy. Physicians, mental health clinics, hospitals, and other health care providers may offer affordable therapies too, in inpatient, outpatient, or residential treatment centers. For addicts in the criminal justice system, the NIDA reported that drug abusers who have been ordered by law to stay in a longer treatment program will recover as well, and sometimes even better, than patients who sought help on their own.[8]

"Toughing it out" alone seldom helps anyone recover from opioid addiction. Therefore, groups such as Narcotics Anonymous, which is based on the successful 12-step program of Alcoholics Anonymous, encourages group members to help one another stay off drugs. Halfway houses funded by governmental agencies, medical groups, or former addicts have also succeeded in helping recovering addicts to form a constructive lifestyle, accept responsibility for their actions, and return to work or school.

LONG-TERM THERAPY AND REHAB

The article "The Changing Face of Opioid Addiction" reported that, from 2000 to 2005, admissions to treatment facilities decreased for heroin addicts but increased for opioid addiction. Between 1999 and 2003, accidental drug poisoning from methadone went up 213% as people began to use that drug for pain medication rather than as part of an opioid treatment program. Therefore, other treatment options have begun to rely on a combination of buprenorphine and naloxone since that duo blocks the effect of other opioids and cannot be readily abused. In addition, buprenorphine/naloxone relieves withdrawal symptoms among outpatients without making the person feel high. Also, the pharmaceutical design prevents the medication from being crushed, snorted, or injected.[9]

Besides treating opioid addiction with medication, other treatments will usually be used during long-term therapy or rehabilitation. For instance, the previously mentioned article "Teen Prescription Drug Abuse" discussed the importance of considering various risk factors while planning an effective course of treatment. If, for example, a patient's records show a pattern of drug abuse, the medical team might focus on causes such as a history of chronic pain, a psychiatric disorder, or even the person's insistence on having a cigarette immediately upon awakening. To find out what would be the most beneficial course of treatment, the medical team may use a screening tool such as "Screener and Opioid Assessment for Patients with Pain" provided on www.painedu.org. If this or another tool shows the existence of two or more risk factors, the patient might best be helped by intervention from two or more health specialties such as psychiatry, pain management, and nutritional counseling. In addition, strong consideration should be given to non-narcotic treatment. Although medication might be needed at first to ease the patient off drugs, prescriptions should be kept to a minimum with no refills provided without a follow-up from the medical team leader or the primary care physician.

The article "Issues in Long-Term Opioid Therapy" in a 2009 issue of *Mayo Clinic Proceedings* discussed other tests such as the Opioid Risk Tool (ORT) that can help a medical team assess the risks involved in treating drug abuse patients. For example, the five-question ORT test asks patients key questions about their personal history, whereas the Screening Instrument for Substance Abuse Potential (SISAP) test has a 24-item questionnaire. In either case, patients rate their frequency of drug abuse and also a variety of mental health issues or antisocial behaviors that may affect a treatment plan.[10]

The same article also talked about the need for ongoing assessment of the "4 A's of pain treatment," which include analgesia (pain), activities of daily living, adverse events (such as a stroke or seizure), and aberrant drug-taking behaviors. The information the patient provides will then be used to plan an appropriate treatment. For example, a patient with aberrant drug-taking behaviors might have been known to crush and snort or inject narcotics meant only to be swallowed. This and other information collected by the medical team can help to determine the most effective treatment for that particular person. In any case, the goal is to tailor a treatment program that will work and will help the drug abuser to become and stay clean, thereby improving the overall quality of life.

An article in the September 2008 issue of the journal *Pain* reported on a study of men and women admitted to treatment for opioid analgesic abuse. More than 60% of those subjects continued to have chronic pain. Indeed, 79%

of the men and 85% of the women said their first exposure to opioids came through a prescription pain reliever. Eventually 60% to 70% of the group misused PPRs to get high, then most of the group later sought treatment for drug abuse, some three or more times. In addition, most of the group also showed signs of very poor health, physically and mentally.[11]

When the risk factors for potential drug abuse can be identified early, an effective treatment will usually be found. Support from other people helps greatly too. For instance, an article on recovery from opioid addiction in the *Journal of Substance Abuse Treatment* reported on the five-year follow-up of 432 admissions to 18 outpatient treatment programs. The study divided the participants into two groups of non-recovering and recovering patients who reported no opioid use, a minimal use of alcohol, and no arrests during the previous year. The 28% in the recovery group said they relied on their own motivations, their experiences in treatment, their religious or spiritual beliefs, their families, and their jobs to help them remain drug free. Since the patients especially emphasized the importance of having the support of close friends and family, the authors of this study concluded that social networks must be established to help any recovering drug addict who lacks those local resources.[12]

A combination of therapies may be the best approach for most drug abusers seeking treatment. For example, behavioral therapy may be added to a recovery plan that includes medications and nutritional support. Treatments can be tailored to the drug abuse patterns of each patient, taking into account any medical, psychiatric, and social problems that must be addressed to prevent the person from lapsing into old habits that first led toward drug abuse. If a relapse does occur, the patient and family members should consider this as they would any chronic disease requiring ongoing treatment or an adjustment in lifestyle. For instance, a patient who has a recurrent medical condition might be in remission for a while but then later require additional treatments or alternate therapies. Similarly a lapse into drug misuse or abuse should be viewed not as a hopeless failure or as a loss of willpower but as a challenge to reconsider all of the available options for that person until a workable treatment can be found.

6
Illegal Use of Prescription Pain Relievers

"What a mess!" Mark said, yet he did not look relieved when Liz and Jon offered to stay to help him clean up. "We've had parties before, and nothing happened, but now . . . do you think Maria will be okay?"

"She had already started to wake up before they got her into the ambulance," Jon reminded him. "Besides, the paramedics said she should be fine."

"Do you think they'll report me to the police?" Mark asked, sounding worried.

Liz shook her head. "Our state has a Good Samaritan law, so anyone can call 911 to help someone who's overdosed without worrying about getting charged."

Mark let out a deep sigh. "That's good, because my parents would ground me for the rest of my life if I got arrested for having all these drugs in the house!"

"Then get rid of them!" Liz said. "They sure didn't help Maria, and they have not helped you."

Mark looked puzzled. "Whoa! You sound ticked! It's not like I'm some drug dealer pushing illegal drugs on street kids!"

"Isn't it?" Liz snapped back. "Just because a doctor wrote a prescription doesn't mean the drugs in this house are being used legally. And you might not be dealing drugs to street kids, but you've given them to the neighbor kids on our street!"

64

Judging by the shocked expression on his face, Mark had never thought of it that way, and neither had Jon. Liz really told him! Jon thought. Then he realized, If I hadn't been talking with Liz and had tried the drugs, I might be in the emergency room now too!

WHERE DO ALL THE DRUGS COME FROM?

Unlike street drugs that often enter the U.S. illegally from other countries or are concocted in someone's basement, prescription pain relievers (PPRs) and over-the-counter (OTC) products usually come from a medicine shelf at home. Prescriptions and OTC drugs can be purchased on the Internet, but most come directly from a local drugstore or the pharmacies often found in large stores and supermarkets, making the drugs readily available to most people. That availability is an important factor since easy access to a drug—any drug—historically influences its current pattern of abuse. Not surprisingly, then, the misuse and abuse of highly accessible products continues to rise.

The report "Prescription for Danger" issued by the Office of National Drug Control Policy in January 2008, stated that 2,500 young people every day between ages 12 and 17 abuse a prescription pain reliever for the first time. Among 12- to 13-year-olds, prescription drugs remain the drug of choice, with OxyContin being a favorite among 12th graders. In addition, about half of the teens who abused those PPRs also admitted to having used two or more other drugs and/or alcohol to get high. Sometimes the alcohol came from a liquor cabinet at home or a friend's house, but some young teens obtained it from the OTC cough remedies they can buy for themselves almost anywhere without worrying about legal consequences or worrying that their parents might find out.

Statistics vary from year to year, but for 2007, the "Prescription for Danger" article reported that about two-thirds (64%) of the teenagers aged 12–17 who admitted that they had misused or abused pain relievers said they got them from friends or relatives. Eight percent reported buying PPRs from someone they knew, and another 10% admitted they just took the drugs without paying for them or asking anyone.

The article "Prescription Opioid Abuse and Dependence," in a 2007 issue of the *Journal of Counseling and Development*, talked about other strategies that teens use to obtain PPRs, such as deceiving a physician or trying to outsmart the whole medical system. For example, a person might go "doctor shopping" to get medications from several physicians, later returning to the doctors they believe are the most gullible. Other common deceptions include making up or exaggerating actual symptoms, lying about drug misuse or the previous abuse of a narcotic, falsely reporting the loss or theft of a medication, stealing a page from a prescription pad, and goading doctors into providing a specific drug or an early refill. Some teens also participated in "pharmacy shopping" where they went from one drugstore to another to avoid suspicions by the pharmacists who refill their medications.[1]

In the article "Young, Assured and Playing Pharmacists to Friends," Amy Harmon discussed a trend among teens who do their own research on a drug, then get a prescription from a doctor who agrees with their recommendation. These "amateur pharmacists" include those who obtain pills from friends or from Internet pharmacies that illegally dispense drugs without a prescription. As Harmon explained, "To some extent, the embrace by young adults of better living through chemistry is driven by familiarity." Unlike earlier generations who may have relied on nutrition, exercise, and OTC products, today's youth have often taken drugs prescribed by their pediatricians or doctors to treat attention deficit disorder (ADD), hyperactivity, depression, insomnia, or anxiety. After a while these teens feel confident in their ability to educate themselves through medical books, journals, and information obtained from the Internet, not only to treat themselves but also to "prescribe" drugs for their friends. Some have been known to lie to their doctors to get medications that they think they or their friends actually need. As "amateur pharmacists" these teens might also trade prescription drugs they no longer take for something they want to try, or they might find ways to get new drugs on the Internet without a prescription.[2]

DISTRIBUTING DRUGS ON THE INTERNET

In the online article "The Possible Dangers of Buying Medicines over the Internet," the Food and Drug Administration (FDA) warned consumers about "rogue Web sites" that sell drugs that have not been checked for safety, effectiveness, and/or consistent amounts of the right ingredients. People ordering from those companies might buy capsules with either too much or too little of the main ingredient, or they might get an illegally manufactured product that has the wrong ingredients altogether. Since some sites sell counterfeits of FDA-approved medications, the products might look like the real thing, and yet the quality and safety of those drugs remain unknown. Some fraudulent sites have even sold contaminated products that caused serious side effects.

The U.S. Drug Enforcement Agency (DEA) reported that rogue sites fill prescriptions with no medical examination and no more information than what they get from an online questionnaire filled out by the potential buyer. These cyber drug sites often show ads for powerful drugs along with a picture of a respectable-looking person dressed like or represented as a doctor or other member of the medical profession who "greets" clients online. Cyber drug dealers also pretend to save people money, but their real interest is getting more money for themselves. For instance, most rogue sites have been designed to find out what narcotics their customers want and how they plan to pay for those drugs. A real doctor, of course, would focus on diagnosing the actual health problem and then finding the best course of medical treatment. Drugs might be part of that treatment, but the legitimate concern of a legitimate doctor will always be the health and well-being of the patient.[3]

The main goal of rogue sites that illegally sell or distribute drugs is to make money, not to help the patient. For instance, a fake pharmacy will seldom have a legitimate phone number or mailing address. The ads may be slick and the Web site well designed, and the prices may entice buyers with "bargains" considerably below the average costs found in well-known chains or discount drugstores. When the products arrive, they may smell, taste, or look different than they should. For instance, the texture might feel odd or the coloration faded, especially if a drug has passed its expiration date. Unsafe storage methods and poor handling or shipping can also cause medications to be too risky to use.

To help consumers know what to look for when they want to buy legal drugs in a legal manner through the Internet, the FDA article offered this advice: Find an Internet pharmacy with headquarters in the United States and with a real pharmacist available online to answer questions. Look for the clear sign of authenticity issued by the National Association of Boards of Pharmacy's (NABP) Verified Internet Pharmacy Practice Sites seal, also known as the VIPPS seal. This means the pharmacy has been licensed by the state in which it operates and also meets other high standards set by the U.S. government. A legitimate pharmacy will require a verifiable prescription from a licensed physician before it ships any PPR or other medication that cannot be bought locally over the counter. Also make sure that the online pharmacy offers secure shopping and promises to protect any personal information collected from the client. When the medication arrives, the FDA further advises consumers, check the drug carefully to see if anything seems unusual or suspicious about the packaging or product.[4]

The illegal sales of legal drugs can happen anywhere, but of course the Internet is everywhere. People can remain anonymous as they provide services for which they have little or no training and no accountability. Customers have advantages, too, as they find a lot of choices or easy payment options to help them place orders quickly. Rogue sites take advantage of this, making cyber drug dealers a primary source for distributing prescription drugs that have been made, bought, or sold in an unlawful manner. The DEA and other governmental agencies continually work to counter these public health threats by passing laws and conducting investigations. They also encourage people in the United States and around the world to help by reporting the unlawful sales of pharmaceutical drugs on the toll-free international hotline, (877) RxAbuse or (877) 792-2873.

SAFELY GETTING RID OF DRUGS

Ironically, getting drugs seems to be less troublesome for teens than getting rid of them. Movie and television stereotypes often portray drug users of all ages frantically flushing narcotics down the toilet as police sirens blare and blue lights flash. However, this might not be the safest way to get rid of drugs that have passed their expiration date or are no longer needed. For example, dumping opioids, other PPRs, and even OTC or nonprescription drugs into a septic tank or a city sewage system can cause small amounts of the narcotics to seep into nearby lakes, rivers, drinking wells, and water systems, potentially harming people, animals, fish, and the plant life found in those wet environments. Although most people and pets will not notice trace amounts of a drug, some medications have cumulative effects that can disturb or mutate the growth of normal body cells and plant cells. Obviously, the disposal of large amount of drugs into a waterway will increase the risk of harming someone or something at some time or another, but frequently dumping small amounts of medications can do that too.

Since the FDA has the official job of worrying about such matters, the agency provides guidelines for disposing PPRs and other medications. It has determined that some medications are safe to flush away. So if the FDA says flush, then flush, because the agency has proven that dissolving the drug in water and washing it down the drain is the best and safest option. Other options, however, will depend on the type of drug and the way in which the medication is usually administered. For example, a skin patch contains active ingredients in the glue, so the safest method of disposing a used or out-of-date patch first requires folding glue against glue to seal in the drug before flushing a toilet-friendly patch. If there's no chance of a young child, curious adolescent, family pet, or anyone else fishing the patch out of the garbage can, however, then it can also be folded, sealed, and safely tossed into the bin.

To get rid of pills and capsules, the safest options generally include these steps:

- Follow the instructions that came with the medication, or ask a reputable licensed pharmacist the best means of disposal.
- Remove the medication from its original container. Scratch off the label or black out any information that might be used to identify and make illegal use of the prescription number, the name of the person, and/or the name of the drug.
- If pharmaceutical instructions do not recommend rinsing the medicine down a drain or flushing it down the toilet, then crush the pills or capsules, being careful not to inhale the dust or powder that may rise. Mix the powder with something as inedible and unappetizing as old cat litter before scooping it into a garbage can. Coffee grounds work, too, assuming the unsavory concoction will go into a trash bag and not a compost pile where ingredients can soak into the soil. Otherwise, outdated or unwanted OTC products can usually be sealed in a plastic bag and tossed into the garbage. But, again, read the packaging instructions to be sure.

If the instructions for any medication are long gone and no local pharmacist can be found on call to ask, the same information can be found on the

Internet. A good starting place, of course, would be the Web site of the manufacturer for that particular drug or the FDA Web site. The FDA also posts a list of drugs that can be flushed on the page "Disposal by Flushing of Certain Unused Medicines." That same Web page suggests asking a local pharmacist about a medical disposal program in the area. For instance, some city or county trash and recycling services provide drug take-back programs where people in the community can remove unwanted or expired medicines from their homes.[5]

DIVERTING PAIN MEDS

In "Prescription for Danger" mentioned earlier, the Office of National Drug Control Policy reported that more than 50% of the teenagers whom they had studied admitted to using PPRs because the drugs themselves are not illegal. About 33% considered PPR use to bring less shame than using illicit drugs, and 21% said their parents did not care as much if they got caught. In addition 56% of the teens said prescription drugs are much easier to obtain than illegal narcotics bought on the street. Therefore, PPRs often get diverted from a legitimate prescription for legitimate pain to an illicit route of buying, selling, misusing, and abusing drugs.

For example, the increased use of methadone to treat pain and to ease opioid addicts through withdrawal symptoms has made this a highly popular drug, not only for doctors to prescribe but for drug traffickers to steal. In the publication "Methadone Diversion, Abuse, and Misuse," the National Drug Intelligence Center reported that thefts usually occur en route from the drug manufacturer to the hospitals, pharmacies, and retail outlets meant to dispense the medication legally. Between 2004 and 2006, the incidents of these thefts went from 28 to 68, with more than 9,000 tablets reported stolen in 2006 alone as supplies were being transported just to methadone clinics.[6]

According to the National Survey on Drug Use and Health (NSDUH), PPRs have been diverted from their intended usage more than any other pharmaceutical drug. The DEA identified the majority of these pain relievers as controlled prescription opioids, especially popular among adolescents and young adults because of the euphoric effect or "high" they deliver. These prescription opioids are not usually distributed through drug trafficking organizations or criminal groups the way heroin and cocaine are, but some illegal distributors on the streets or in motorcycle gangs have diverted controlled prescription drugs (CPD) to their supplies of illegally obtained narcotics. Crime remains higher with the usage of illicit drugs for which no prescription is available, but in the past five years, CPD diversion has caused a rise in violence and property crimes in all areas of the United States. This in turn has added to the burden of already stressed law enforcement agencies, drug treatment centers, health insurance programs, and other resources meant to help and protect the well-being of the general public.[7]

Diverting legal drugs to illegal uses also has a way of diverting many young people from normal lives into social problems and criminal pursuits. For example, the U.S. Department of Health and Human Services reported that, in 2008, 15.9% of the 12- to 17-year-olds who had misused prescription drugs in the previous month had also gotten into a serious fight at work or school. Approximately 40% of the youth who admitted to using illicit drugs admitted they had stolen or tried to steal items worth $50 or more. Of the young adults already on parole or in a supervised release program from jail, 27.8% said they continued to be dependent on at least one drug.[8]

THE LEGAL CONSEQUENCES OF ILLEGAL DRUG ACTIVITIES

Many states are now considering or have recently passed a Good Samaritan bill to encourage people to phone 911 to get emergency help for a drug overdose victim without worrying about being charged themselves for drug possession. Likewise, the victim will not be charged for possessing narcotics. However, this legislation will not void any outstanding warrants nor avoid the legal woes, further investigations, or arrests of anyone suspected of manufacturing or distributing the drugs found on the scene.

Controlled substances get controlled for a reason: These drugs have been proven to have beneficial effects such as the relief of pain, but they have also been shown to be highly addictive. Often that occurs, as it does with PPRs, because of the medication's effect on the central nervous system. Since those effects and their consequences are not something to play around with, state monitoring systems have been set into place to make sure that doctors, pharmacists, veterinarians, nurse practitioners, and other medical persons do not sell or distribute a legal drug in an illegal manner.

A NEW MODEL IN NEW MEXICO

In 2003 more than twice as many people died from narcotic overdose in New Mexico than anywhere else in the country. Those narcotics included illicit drugs such as heroin, but, from 1995 to 2004, accidental deaths caused by overdosing on prescription medications increased 362%. Why? No one wanted to call 911! Reportedly, even friends and family who were afraid of being arrested for possessing drugs themselves did not call, or they waited until all attempts to revive the person had failed. Unfortunately those calls for help came too late. Multiple studies of overdose episodes show that people rarely die immediately after a drug-related overdose. Most deaths occur 1 to 3 hours after the first drug dosage, long after the amount of time an emergency medical team typically needs to arrive on a scene and respond with life-saving care.[9]

With one person dying from a drug overdose every day in New Mexico, state legislators agreed that something had to be done—and fast! In 2001 the state passed the Overdose Prevention and Response Program, supervised by the New Mexico Department of Health, to train drug users, their families, and friends how to recognize the symptoms of an overdose while also protecting those who call 911 to save the life of an overdose victim. Now seen as a national model for other states that have not yet passed a Good Samaritan bill, the New Mexico program demonstrates how educational information and public health responses can reduce drug fatalities and save the lives of family members and friends.

By January 2010, **prescription drug monitoring** programs (PDMP) had gone into effect in more than 30 states. These programs help to educate doctors, medical specialists, and the general public. While protecting client confidentiality, PDMP databases help doctors and pharmacists find out quickly if prescriptions are being abused. They also help law enforcement agencies to identify potential problems, prevent prescription drug abuse, and keep legally prescribed drugs from being diverted into illegal sales and uses.[10]

According to information from the National Conference of State Legislatures (NCSL), PDMPs allow medical professionals to log each prescription they write or fill into a state database, which they can also access for their own information. This helps physicians and pharmacists to prevent drug misusers or potential abusers from getting prescriptions from multiple doctors or pharmacies. Besides helping directly, PDMP helps indirectly by reducing the availability or accessibility of prescription drugs. As PPRs become harder to get, they're less likely to be diverted or abused.[11]

Despite the safeguards, some PPRs continue to be redirected into illegal use. Laws exist, for example, to make it illegal to distribute any drug, including PPRs, without the proper labels, carefully sealed packaging, and FDA-approved instructions—any or all of which would be difficult to counterfeit. Although most teenagers would not attempt a federal offense, many do tempt local authorities into catching them for a "drug, narcotic, or chemical offense," defined by the DEA as "the possession, distribution, manufacture, cultivation, sale, transfer, or the attempt or conspiracy" to do any of the above. For example, under Section 844, "Penalties for simple possession," a person who obtained a controlled substance by a means other than a prescription can be fined at least $1,000 and jailed for up to a year. That's assuming, of course, that this is the first offense for simple possession. If not, the penalties more than double and continue to go up from there.

Importing, exporting, or selling drug paraphernalia carries stiffer penalties, but this usually involves illicit drugs rather than legally prescribed medications. A more likely occurrence among teens would be someone who has stockpiled an abundance of PPRs, which they then sell or distribute to minors like themselves. If, however, the person with the drugs is 18 or older and distributes those drugs to anyone under 21, the maximum penalty doubles for the first offense and triples for the second. Similar penalties exist for anyone who distributes a drug near school property, playgrounds, youth centers, and pretty much anywhere that children are most likely to be found.[12]

7
Reviving the Future

For a while after Tom's party, Brendan barely saw Tom at school. When they finally ran into each other, Tom seemed ill at ease. Someone in the neighborhood had asked his parents why paramedics had come to the house while they were away, so it did not take them long to find out their son been hosting a pharm party. The local authorities let Tom off that night since he was underage, but he had to tell his parents everything. "Man, did I get grounded!" he told Brendan. Then he asked, "Did you get in trouble too?"

Brendan shook his head. "I could honestly tell my folks I did not do any drugs that night, and they believed me."

"That's a relief," Tom said, flashing a quick smile. For a moment he looked like himself again, but the lightness dropped away as soon as he asked Brendan about Gina.

"I think she'll be okay—maybe better than okay if she keeps going to counseling after she gets out of rehab," Brendan said. "I guess she actually needed some medical help, too, and I can already tell a difference. I mean, I wouldn't exactly call her happy, but she's not freaked out about everything like she's been ever since her mother left."

Tom sighed. "Good. I thought about calling, but I didn't know what to say."

Brendan laughed. "Don't worry about that. Gina is never at a loss for words, and she's just glad to know anybody cares. Her foster mom and counselor told Hannah and me that calls and visits help a lot, so we've been phoning or dropping by."

THE IMPORTANCE OF CONTINUING THERAPY

In a drug therapy treatment program, a big problem that people must leave behind concerns expectations—either their own or someone else's. The more unrealistic those expectations, the more they can hinder recovery. For instance, the Centers for Disease Control and Prevention (CDC) Web site pointed out two commonly believed myths that frequently get in the way:

1. Therapy helps most addicts to become completely drug-free.
2. If addicts really, really want to quit doing drugs, they can stop by themselves.

When those expectations prove untrue, however, many patients become discouraged from trying again.

In both myths, one flaw is a belief that drug abuse is a voluntary action or a deliberate decision, which then makes the success of a treatment program dependent on the patient's willpower, motivation, or strength to overcome a weakness in character. Another flaw has to do with thinking that a drug addict can recover alone. But, as the CDC pointed out, no one places those expectations on patients recovering from other types of addiction. Consider, for example, the difficulties that family, friends, and the general public expect smokers to face as they try to quit smoking. The addictive nature of nicotine and the difficulties of quitting have been accepted and understood by most people, so no one seems surprised when only 3% to 7% of the smokers who try to quit each year succeed. Instead smokers are encouraged to try again and often urged to take a new approach, whether that be nicotine patches, gum, hypnosis, antidepressants, or acupuncture. This public view also lets smokers know they are not alone in their difficult decision. Other people are standing by and may have "been there" too.

Society also seems to accept the fact that every illness or problem cannot be cured. Relapses occur. Diets get forgotten. Medications don't always work well, and therapies do not always have the desired effect in bringing about a healthier lifestyle. In any of those situations, a patient who also has a mental health problem may find a successful recovery or even some type of improvement much harder to obtain.

To ease the generally harsher expectations placed on drug addicts who are trying to recover, the CDC made these important points:

- Addiction affects brain chemistry and brain cells. The longer a person has been on drugs, the more likely it becomes that the structure and functions of the brain have changed. These alterations make a normal brain abnormal, causing compulsions, cravings, and a dependency on drugs.
- Addiction has many facets. As the CDC put it, this "biobehavioral disorder" affects the mental, physical, and emotional health of the patient and also affects the family, community, peers, and friends.
- Drug addiction is a chronic disease that may not be curable, but it is treatable. If too many changes in the brain have occurred for too long, a "cure" may not be a realistic goal, but substance abuse treatments can continue successfully on many levels, depending on the person and the multiple facets of addiction that must be addressed.

As drug addicts and their families or friends strive for workable goals and realistic expectations, some changes in vocabulary may help to change the general way of thinking. For example, the idea of being "in recovery" works better than assessing if a person has or has not recovered. With the more realistic concept of an ongoing process, the goal of eliminating drug use forever can be changed to the more manageable "one day at a time."

Using a variety of approaches, patients can effectively set reasonable, achievable goals such as reducing drug use, avoiding criminal activities, finishing school, holding down a job, and working toward a stable life. As the CDC discovered, a number of factors will help to make those goals a reality, beginning with the need to make drug therapy programs available to everyone for an adequate amount of time. For example, an outpatient or residential program that finishes in less than 90 days will seldom be as effective as, say, a one-year program that provides enough hours for addicts to address all of the issues that need to be considered. Given adequate time, though, a workable treatment can be developed for each individual with adjustments made as needed during the course of therapy. For instance, those with mental health issues may need long-term counseling sessions and those with chemical changes in the brain may need medical treatment to correct the changes. Medications may need to be adjusted and diets reevaluated with appropriate changes in goals and expectations occasionally needed as well.[1]

DRUG TESTS

Some parents, some schools, and most employers, including the various branches of the U.S. Armed Forces, may require drug tests, especially if a recovering addict has been in trouble with the law. Students do not usually support a drug habit costing hundreds of dollars each month (sometimes per week) with a paycheck from their part-time employment in a fast-food restaurant. Since the high expense of drugs must be covered somehow, the monies often come from stealing or from selling narcotics, including PPRs, to other drug users. To prevent these crimes, workplace drug testing can be a condition of employment. Often such tests begin with urine analysis, although some drug-testing programs analyze a strand of the patient's hair since this method shows drugs in the system much longer—up to 90 days. Tests rarely rely on blood samples, though, since this invasive method requires a needle, which most drug testers avoid.[2]

Attempts to cheat on a drug test are not uncommon, however. For instance, some users have been known to dilute a urine sample or drink lots of liquid just before a drug test, thinking this will water down the results. Others have tried adding something to the urine sample, not realizing that vinegar, apple juice, or other similarly colored products mainly change the pH balance, thereby assuring the person that the next urine test will be under same-sex supervision. Substituting body fluids from someone else seldom works either, since the specimen will not pass temperature markers in on-site tests. If, however, the person has to go to a local lab or clinic, other safeguards will be put into place. For instance, the water in the toilet may be colorized, and coats, bags, backpacks, or other devices used for concealing fake samples will not be allowed in the collection area. So potential cheaters will be caught either during the test or by the results from the lab, which, again, means that the next test will be supervised by someone of the same sex.[3]

In the U.S. Navy, finding a same-sex supervisor would not be hard to do and may be likely. Ever since a drug-related episode in the early 1980s brought to light a drug problem described by the Department of Defense as being of "epic proportions," the navy has focused on drug abuse prevention. Its goal is not to catch drug users but to prevent drug use. Apparently the navy's efforts have begun to pay off. An article in *Stars and Stripes* reported that in 2001 more than 6,000 sailors tested positive for drugs found in more than 900,000 samples. By 2008, only 2,120 sailors tested drug-positive out of 1.9 million tested. Active service members of the air force had the lowest incidents of drug use, and the U.S. Army the highest with the Marines in between, but the navy has not been deterred from its target of zero drug use. To do this, it plans to stay aware of popular trends, increase drug-testing programs, and monitor such items as OTC medicines with a potential for abuse. In addition, naval commands of 500 members or more have now been assigned drug counselors and alcohol advisers as a permanent part of the team.[4]

But that's the navy. Do administrators have the right to hold random drug tests in junior and senior high schools? According to a Supreme Court ruling, yes, they do, at least among students who participate in school-sponsored sports events or other competitive activities. Teens whose parents or guardians have consented to testing may be randomly tested too. The idea is not to punish the students but to discourage young people from beginning drug use and also to identify the teens who already need drug counseling or other types of therapeutic treatment.

ANTIDRUG PROGRAMS

In his 2003 State of the Union address, President George W. Bush announced the Access To Recovery (ATR) initiative on behalf of the U.S. government. This program expands substance abuse treatments, increases the number of providers, and gives clients more choices in their own recovery through a voucher system to be used in developing an individual plan of treatment. ATR includes faith-based facilities and practical support through such services as transportation, mentoring, and child care. In addition, ATR allows each state and tribal organization to tailor programs to the needs of its people. In Texas, for instance, the criminal justice system needed more drug treatment facilities, while other states needed to focus on particular drugs being used.

The U.S. National Drug Control Strategy, which provided the above information, reported that the United States has historically had one of the highest rates of drug abuse in the world. As a result, the United States gathered its resources to learn about the nature of addiction, the ways to prevent drug abuse, and workable treatments that show the most positive effects on individuals and the communities in which they live. Since many other countries now have drug abuse problems, the United States offers "cost-effective, research-tested . . . initiatives that have proven successful in the United States and could be helpful to countries around the world in addressing their own drug abuse challenges." These initiatives particularly highlight the importance of:

- launching antidrug media campaigns aimed toward youth
- building alliances within local communities
- beginning drug testing in schools and workplaces
- screening for drugs and intervening in cycles of drug abuse
- providing affordable but high-quality treatment services
- establishing drug treatment courts

Based on science and research, the antidrug programs aim to "deliver clear, consistent, credible, and sustained anti-drug messages" in the hope of keeping kids off drugs. Random drug testing has that aim, too: not only to discourage drug usage but also to assist teens in getting help before their misuse of drugs has time to damage brain cells or progress into habitual drug abuse. Similarly, screening tools such as questionnaires may be used to help teens realize they need help. In the United States alone, the National Survey on Drug Use and Health estimated that more than 20 million people fit a medical definition of addiction or abuse, and yet more than 94% do not even know they have a problem. Those who do may already be either in a treatment program or in jail.

For nonviolent drug offenders, drug courts join the power of the justice system with effective treatment programs intended to break the cycle of criminal behavior that often occurs with drug use, child abuse or neglect, and incarceration. Since the inception of the first drug court in Miami, Florida, in 1989, the goal has been to stop substance abuse as well as the criminal behavior that often accompanies addiction. To do this, the court may dismiss or lower the original charges or offer a reduced sentence upon the completion of a drug treatment program. To further encourage successful treatments, some courts meet on the grounds of residential drug rehab centers, so that transportation will pose no problem for patients.

With more than a decade of drug court research now available, the evidence shows excellent outcomes. For instance, a national study showed that 43.3% of the drug offenders who did not have a hearing in a drug court would be charged with a serious offense within a year of graduation from a treatment program, whereas only 16.4% of the drug court graduates were arrested in that first year. These encouraging results have now helped to establish more than 2,000 drug courts in the United States, with similar facilities now opened in 10 other countries.[5]

PREVENTING ADDICTION

Educating children, teens, parents, and the general public to the dangers of misusing and abusing drugs can be done by schools, health clinics, and religious centers within the community. However, the *Clinician Reviews* article "Teen Prescription Drug Abuse" pointed out that 21% of teenagers admit to misusing prescription pain medicines, and yet only 1% of the parents considered it "extremely likely" or even "very likely" that *their* child had done this. When parents address the issue or actively participate in teaching their children about the dangers of PPR misuse and abuse, the article said, the numbers of drug incidents could be cut in half. Drug companies and medical professionals can also do their part. As the article suggested, writing out the number of pills on handwritten prescriptions and using watermark protection for online prescriptions helps to cut down forgeries. Those processes also keep rogue sites from diverting legal drugs into illicit cyber drug markets.

In addition to those workable solutions, the article "Can Abuse Deterrent Formulations Make a Difference?" in *Harm Reduction Journal* said that changing the formulation of a drug can deter abusers from crushing, dissolving, melting, smoking, and injecting it. Although this won't keep anyone from swallowing too many pills, they will be prevented from taking drugs in ways known to bump up the high. That alone will make the products less desirable for recreational use, and will also keep abusers from sharing needles that inject HIV, hepatitis, and other blood-borne diseases that shorten lives but lengthen the list of public health concerns in the United States.

Not surprisingly, preventative plans work best when they focus on people between the ages of 11 and 13, since adolescents are most likely to experiment with drugs during those years. Training older teenagers to help young kids resist peer pressure can be highly effective too, but nothing replaces the positive influence of stable, loving families who openly discuss their social standards and values. Nevertheless, friends, teachers, and caregivers within a community can encourage children and teens to make wise choices and to behave responsibly at work and school. Encouraging youth to find constructive and creative ways to cope with stress helps to build self-control and a positive self-image.

Health providers, pharmacists, and primary care physicians also have important roles in preventing addiction. For example, the National Institute on Drug Abuse suggested that doctors can use regular checkups to ask patients questions about drug use, and they can be aware of any signs suggesting a potential problem. Likewise, pharmacists who fill prescriptions can take care to advise patients on the dangers of opioid-based medications and warn of potential **drug interactions**. Pharmacists can also join the first line of defense in recognizing various signs of abuse. For instance, a client might have PPR prescriptions from more than one doctor, indicating signs of doctor shopping, or a pharmacist might be the first to suspect a forged prescription.[6]

In their zeal to stop abuse or prevent drug addiction, some concerned citizens have been known to overdo. For example, Supreme Court justices ruled 8 to 1 that school authorities had overstepped their authority when they ordered a 13-year-old girl to be strip-searched by a school nurse to see if she had hidden ibuprofen in her bra or panties. She had not. Despite the young teen's humiliation, school officials defended their search as a necessary means of combating a growing problem with drugs. The Supreme Court, however, upheld the constitutional right of every citizen, regardless of age, to be protected from such an unreasonable search and seizure.[7]

TREATING ACTUAL PAIN

Whether over-the-counter or prescription strength, ibuprofen and aspirin may be part of a doctor-prescribed plan to treat actual incidents of pain. One opioid-free medication that has recently been approved by the FDA is an injectable form of ibuprofen, currently used only in hospitals to treat pain or fever. A clinical trial showed that patients who received injections after surgery were less likely to use the morphine pump available to them as needed.[8]

For many people, regular capsules or tablets of ibuprofen, aspirin, or other OTC pain relievers can lessen pain effectively with no need for opioid drugs. When misused, though, even aspirin and acetaminophen can cause adverse side effects ranging from a stomachache to drug poisoning. Therefore, the FDA has continued to work to educate the public by providing numerous resources and medical updates that inform people about the drugs they take. For instance, the FDA Web page "Find the Latest Drug Product and Safety Information" has an index to drug-specific information and also links to public health advisories, a drug safety newsletter, consumer health information, and even drug safety podcasts, all of which help people to search for up-to-date information on PPRs and other drugs.[9] The FDA site also includes information about the status of new drugs, as well as data about older medications. The Web page called "Medication Guides" provides the same kind of information found on those paper inserts that come inside each packaged drug.[10]

For some time a common practice in pain management has been to use a long-acting opioid to control chronic pain and a second, short-acting pain reliever to treat occasional breakthrough pain. This method often helps a patient to feel less discomfort and to function normally. However, patients who have misused or abused opioids need another course of pain management therapy. For some this means more than medication.

The National Institutes of Health addressed a variety of options when they created the National Center for Complementary and Alternative Medicine (NCCAM) Web site. For example, the Web page "Take Charge of Your Health" provides links to alternative pain management treatments such as herbs and acupuncture. A search for "pain relief" on the NCCAM site also brings up such topics as spinal manipulation, massage therapy, and magnets to ease pain.

Do these options work? For some, they do. For others, the test results have not yet arrived. At this writing, for example, the National Cancer Institute has begun a study on using magnetic acupressure to reduce pain in cancer patients whose treatments include tests that often increase pain.[11]

Medical News Today published the online article "Electroacupuncture Shows Effects on Pain Perception," which reported on the pain-reducing effects of electrical current applied through acupuncture needles. Patients who received the treatment for 20 and 40 minutes had less relief from pain than those who were given the treatment for 30 minutes. Therefore, further studies will be needed to show why the 30-minute sessions provided the most noticeable effects on pain.[12]

Although acupuncture can be a highly effective tool in managing pain, needles pierce the skin, making this an invasive treatment although minimally so. The technique of acupressure, however, locates and uses the same sites as acupuncture but the practitioner applies pressure rather than needles. This option for pain management can be especially helpful in children and teens with chronic pain or the acute pain that typically follows surgery. Such methods have been used in Eastern cultures for thousands of years, but Western medicine has only recently begun to take these options seriously, often with innovative results. For instance, an article in ScienceDaily reported on the successful use of acupressure beads placed on the forehead of patients aged 8 to 17 to calm the children just before surgery. This form of pain management is inexpensive and noninvasive, and in addition the researchers noticed a drop in the anxiety levels of the children within a half hour.[13]

Another ScienceDaily article, "Therapy Helps Children and Teenagers in Pain," reported on a new pain management option called Acceptance and Commitment Therapy (ACT), a type of behavioral therapy. With ACT and the help of their therapists, young patients establish long-term goals and talk about the consequences of letting chronic pain control their lives. For instance, children and teens might be encouraged to think through and then talk through any situations they tend to avoid because they fear the risk of increasing pain. According to the results of these studies, patients who participated in ACT therapy experienced less pain and less anxiety about taking part in normal activities than did the children and teens who did not have that treatment. Even when actual pain continued, ACT patients learned to function better in their daily lives.[14]

In deciding on a course of treatment for either pain management or drug addiction, medical teams and patients need to work together to find a balance that helps to stabilize the whole person—mentally, physically, and spiritually. Similarly, law enforcement agencies continue to aim toward a healthy balance. In the effort to curb drug abuse among patients and drug trafficking among people who have easy access to drugs, state policies have sometimes created barriers between doctors and their patients. For instance, the Medscape article "Laws and Regulations Governing Pain Relief with Opioids" reported that some state policies hinder physicians from adequately treating pain because they fear they will be blamed if the patient becomes addicted to opioids or other PPRs. The article further reported that some state policies overstep the line by placing limits on the amount of opioids a doctor can prescribe. Or the policies prevent physicians from prescribing opioids unless other options have failed. These examples indicate that several states have limited highly trained physicians from doing their jobs. When kept in balance, though, state policies do not take over the responsibility of medically determining what treatments should be given or for whom. Instead, a well-balanced policy will distinguish between addiction and a physical dependence on drugs needed to treat pain. Such policies will also recognize that the amount of medication given or the length of time taken does not decide whether or not the PPR is needed.[15]

The "Balanced Pain Policy Initiative" initiated by the Center for Practical Bioethics defined pain management as "the core of the covenant between physicians and patients." Several factors such as the lack of education in the medical community and governmental campaigns to prevent the abuse of PPRs and other controlled substances have thrown the covenant out of balance. This makes doctors reluctant to prescribe pain medications and gives patients no relief from pain even though treatments may be available. To restore balance, the pain policy initiative includes two phases. The first began in 2006 to focus research on the administrative and criminal actions taken against physicians, and the second put those findings into use. The initiative brought together a variety of medical organizations to develop and advance a series of programs designed to help primary care providers promote better pain management throughout the United States.[16]

Meanwhile, medical researchers continue to look for other ways to treat pain. For instance, an online article posted in Medical News Today discussed the "Genetic Link Between Physical Pain and Social Rejection." According to the findings of this research, the expression "rejection hurts" may be scientifically proven true. For this study, researchers gave participants a survey to measure and report their sensitivity to personal rejection. In addition, participants were first included, then excluded from social activities. With **magnetic resonance imaging (MRI)** used to study the results, individuals who showed more sensitivity to physical pain also experienced higher levels of sensitivity to social rejection. The tests also showed that certain areas of the brain perceive hurt as hurt without necessarily distinguishing between emotional and physical pain. Of course, most teens who have been ignored by someone they care about or excluded from a group or been the last one picked for a team could have told them that. Most teenagers know that pain of any kind is pain.[17]

Notes

Chapter 1

1. Nora D. Volkow, "Prescription Drugs Abuse and Addiction," Research Report, National Institute on Drug Abuse, revised 2005. Available online. URL: http://www.drugabuse. gov/ResearchReports/ Prescription/Prescription. html. Last updated July 29, 2009.
2. Ibid.
3. Drug News, "Prescription Medicine Abuse: A Serious Problem," Partnership for a Drug-Free America. Available online. URL: http://www.drugfree.org/ Portal/DrugIssue/Features/ Prescription_Medicine_Misuse. Posted September 24, 2008.
4. Leonard J. Paulozzi, "Trends in Unintentional Drug Poisoning Deaths," statement presented before the Energy and Commerce Committee Subcommittee on Oversight and Investigations, U.S. House of Representatives, October 24, 2007. Available online. URL: http://www.hhs.gov/asl/ testify/2007/10/t20071024a. html. Last revised on June 16, 2009.
5. Allison Gandey, "Misuse of Prescription Drugs Rising in the U.S," *Medscape Medical News,* published September 8, 2008. Available online with log-in. URL: http://www.medscape.com/ viewarticle/580158.

Chapter 2

1. Ryan J. Huxtable and Stephan K.W. Schwarz, "The Isolation of Morphine—First Principles in Science and Ethics," *Molecular Interventions* 1 (2001): pp. 189–191.
2. Stephen Harding, Lee Ann Olivier, and Olivera Jokic. "Victorian Substance Abuse," Victorians' Secret. 2000. Available online. URL: http://drugs.uta. edu/drugs.html. Downloaded September 22, 2009.
3. Staff, "Dr. Francis Rynd, Irish Inventor of the Hypodermic Needle and Syringe," Our Ireland. Available online.

URL: http://our-ireland.
com/articles/irish-inventors/
dr-francis-rynd-irish-inventor-
of-the-hypodermic-needle-
and-syringe/. Downloaded
September 22, 2009.

4. Christine Ball and Rod West-
horpe, "Intravenous Equipment: The Beginning of Things,"
Anaesthesia and Intensive Care
28, no.1 (February 2000): p. 3.

5. Alexander Tomov, Anna
Elliott, Ariana Petersen, et al.
"History Affects Morphine:
The Hypodermic Needle," The
Role of Chemistry in His-
tory, published April 30th,
2008. Available online. URL:
http://itech.dickinson.edu/
chemistry/?p=795. Down-
loaded September 22, 2009.

6. Philip J. Hilts, "The FDA at
Work: Cutting-Edge Science
Promoting Public Health,"
FDA Consumer, January–
February 2006. Available
online. URL: http://www.fda.
gov/AboutFDA/WhatWeDo/
History/Overviews/
ucm109801.htm. Downloaded
September 25, 2009.

7. "Milestones of Drug Regulation in the United States,"
U.S. Food and Drug Admin-
istration, updated June
18, 2009. Available online.
URL: http://www.fda.gov/
AboutFDA/WhatWeDo/

History/FOrgsHistory/CDER/
CenterforDrugEvaluationa
ndResearchBrochureandCh
ronology/ucm114463.htm.
Downloaded September 25,
2009.

8. "FDA Takes Actions on
Darvon, Other Pain Medications Containing Propoxy-
phene," U.S. Food and Drug
Administration. Available
online. URL: http://www.fda.
gov/NewsEvents/Newsroom/
PressAnnouncements/
ucm170769.htm. Posted July 7,
2009.

9. MedWatch, "Reporting by
Consumers," The FDA Safety
Information and Adverse Event
Reporting Program, U.S. Depart-
ment of Health and Human
Services. Available online. URL:
http://www.fda.gov/Safety/
MedWatch/HowToReport/
ucm053074.htm. Downloaded
September 29, 2009.

10. "Guidance for Industry
Consumer-Directed Broadcast
Advertisements," U.S. Department of Health and Human
Services. Available online. URL:
http://prescriptiondrugs.procon.
org/sourcefiles/guidance_for_
industry_1999.pdf. Down-
loaded October 2, 2009.

11. ProCon.org, "Should Prescription Drugs Be Advertised
Directly to Consumers?"

Prescription Drug Ads. Available online. URL: http://prescriptiondrugs.procon.org. Downloaded October 2, 2009.

Chapter 3

1. NIDA for Teens: Facts on Drugs, "Brain & Addiction: The Science Behind Drug Abuse," National Institute on Drug Abuse. Available online. URL: http://teens.drugabuse.gov/facts/facts_brain1.php. Downloaded November 2, 2009.

2. C. Tiruppathi, "Opioid Analgesic Drugs," handout for class lecture, Department of Pharmacology, University of Illinois at Chicago. Available online. URL: http://www.uic.edu/classes/pcol/pcol331/dentalpharmhandouts2006/lecture51.pdf. Downloaded October 27, 2009.

3. Gardiner Harris, "Ban Is Advised on 2 Top Pills for Pain Relief," *The New York Times*, published June 30, 2009. Available online. URL: http://www.nytimes.com/2009/07/01/health/01fda.html. Downloaded November 3, 2009.

4. OHS Health & Safety Services; "How Long Do Drugs Stay in Your System?" Health Tests Direct. Available online. URL: http://www.ohsinc.com/how_long_do_drugs_stay_in_your_system.htm. Downloaded October 29, 2009.

5. Caroline Cassels, "Opioid Overdose Triples in the United States, CDC Report Shows," Medscape Medical News, September 30, 2009. Available online. URL: http://www.medscape.com/viewarticle/709744. Downloaded November 3, 2009.

6. Diane Murphy, "Giving Medication to Children," Consumer Updates, Food and Drug Administration. Last updated on July 22, 2009. Available online. URL: http://www.fda.gov/ForConsumers/ConsumerUpdates/ucm164427.htm. Downloaded October 29, 2009.

7. "Food and Drug Administration (FDA) Shelf-Life Extension Program," U.S. Army Medical Materiel Agency. Available online. URL: http://www.usamma.army.mil/dod_slep.cfm. Downloaded October 30, 2009.

8. J.S. Taylor et al., "Stability Profiles of Drug Products Extended Beyond Labeled Expiration Dates," 2002 FDA Science Forum, Board AC-08. Last updated on June 27, 2009. Available online. URL: http://www.accessdata.fda.

gov/ScienceForums/forum02/
AC-08.htm. Downloaded
October 30, 2009.

Chapter 4

1. Alan I. Leshner, "Why Do
   Sally and Johnny Use Drugs?"
   National Institute of Drug
   Abuse. Available online. URL:
   http://www.nida.nih.gov/
   Published_Articles/Sally.html.
   Downloaded November 11,
   2009.

2. National Institute of Drug
   Abuse, "The Brain's Response
   to Drugs," Teachers Guide, NIH
   Publication No. 05-3592, revi-
   sion May 2005. Available online.
   URL: http://teens.drugabuse.
   gov/mom/teachguide/
   MOMTeacherGuide.pdf.
   Downloaded November 2,
   2009.

3. PDR Health, "Drug Abuse,"
   Physicians' Desktop Reference.
   Available online. URL: http://
   www.pdrhealth.com/disease/
   disease-mono.aspx?content
   FileName=BHG01PS06.xml
   &contentName=Drug+Abuse
   &contentId=41&TypeId=1.
   Downloaded November 3,
   2009.

4. Joanna Saisan, Jeanne Segal,
   and Deborah Cutter, "Drug
   Abuse and Addiction,"
   Helpguide.org. Last modified in
   January 2009. Available online.
   URL: http://www.helpguide.
   org/mental/drug_substance_
   abuse_addiction_signs_effects_
   treatment.htm. Downloaded
   November 10, 2009.

5. "OxyContin May Hook Teens
   More Easily than Adults,"
   Reuters Health, September
   17, 2008. Available online.
   URL: http://www.reuters.
   com/article/healthNews/
   idUSCOL77105020080917.
   Downloaded November 20,
   2009.

6. Trevor Bennett, "Decision-
   Making Approach to Opioid Addiction," Center for
   Problem-Oriented Policing. Available online. URL:
   http://www.popcenter.
   org/library/reading/PDFs/
   ReasoningCriminal/06_bennet.
   pdf. Downloaded November
   19, 2009.

7. Li-Tzy Wu et al., "Prescription Pain Reliever Abuse and
   Dependence Among Adolescents: A Nationally Represen-
   tative Study," *Journal of the
   American Academy of Child
   and Adolescent Psychiatry*,
   September 2009. Available
   online through NIH Public
   Access. URL: http://www.
   pubmedcentral.nih.gov/article
   render.fcgi?artid=2636856.
   Downloaded November 19,
   2009.

Chapter 5

1. WebMD, "Drug Overdose," Emedicinehealth.com. Available online. URL: http://www.emedicinehealth.com/drug_overdose/article_em.htm. Downloaded January 11, 2010.

2. "Acetaminophen Poisoning," The Merck Manuals Online Medical Library. Last full review/revision April 2009 by Gerald F. O'Malley, D.O. Available online. URL: http://www.merck.com/mmpe/sec21/ch326/ch326c.html. Downloaded January 12, 2010.

3. "Overdose," MedlinePlus. Available online. URL: http://www.nlm.nih.gov/medlineplus/ency/article/007287.htm. Downloaded January 12, 2010.

4. "Drug Abuse First Aid," MedlinePlus. Available online. URL: http://www.nlm.nih.gov/medlineplus/ency/article/000016.htm. Downloaded January 11, 2010.

5. "Substance Abuse Treatment for Injection Drug Users: A Strategy with Many Benefits," Centers for Disease Control and Prevention. Available online. URL: http://www.cdc.gov/idu/facts/Treatment.htm. Downloaded January 18, 2010.

6. "Abrupt Opioid Withdrawal Increases Pain Sensitivity," Medical News Today. Available online. URL: http://www.medicalnewstoday.com/articles/157258.php. Downloaded January 18, 2010.

7. "Drug Court Fact Sheet: Methadone Maintenance and Other Pharmacotherapeutic Interventions in the Treatment of Opioid Dependence," American Association for the Treatment of Opioid Dependence. Available online. URL: http://www.aatod.org/fact_drug_court.html. Downloaded January 14, 2010.

8. "Principles of Drug Addiction Treatment: A Research Based Guide," National Institute on Drug Abuse, revised April 2009. Available online. URL: http://www.drugabuse.gov/PODAT/PODATIndex.html. Downloaded January 14, 2010.

9. Marilyn H. Bryne, Laura Lander, and Martha Ferris, "The Changing Face of Opioid Addiction," *Health & Social Work* 34, no. 1 (February 2009): pp. 53–56.

10. Steven D. Passik, "Issues in Long-Term Opioid Therapy: Unmet Needs, Risks, and Solutions," *Mayo Clinic Proceedings* 84, no.7 (July 2009): p. 593(9).

11. Theodore J. Cicero, Michael Lynskey, Alexandre Todorov, et al., "Co-morbid Pain and Psychopathology in Males and Females Admitted to Treatment for Opioid Analgesic Abuse," *Pain* 139, no.1 (September 30, 2008): p. 127.

12. Patrick M. Flynn, George W. Joe, Kirk M. Broome, et al. "Recovery from Opioid Addiction in DATOS," *Journal of Substance Abuse Treatment* 25 (Oct. 2003): pp. 177–186.

Chapter 6

1. Daniel J. Weigel, et al. "Prescription Opioid Abuse and Dependence: Assessment Strategies for Counselors," *Journal of Counseling and Development* 85 (2007): pp. 211–215.

2. Amy Harmon, "Young, Assured and Playing Pharmacists to Friends," *The New York Times*, published November 16, 2005. Available online. URL: http://www.nytimes.com/2005/11/16/health/16patient.html?_r=1&hp. Downloaded November 19, 2009.

3. Joseph T. Rannazzisi, "DEA Congressional Testimony," May 16, 2007, U.S. Drug Enforcement Administration. Available online. URL: http://www.justice.gov/dea/pubs/cngrtest/ct051607.html. Downloaded January 22, 2010.

4. "The Possible Dangers of Buying Medicines over the Internet," U.S. Food and Drug Administration. Last updated August 31, 2009. Available online. URL: http://www.fda.gov/ForConsumers/ConsumerUpdates/ucm048396htm. Downloaded January 19, 2010.

5. "Disposal by Flushing of Certain Unused Medicines: What You Should Know," U.S. Food and Drug Administration. Available online. URL: http://www.fda.gov/Drugs/ResourcesForYou/Consumers/BuyingUsingMedicineSafely/EnsuringSafeUseofMedicine/SafeDisposalofMedicines/ucm186187.htm. Downloaded January 22, 2010.

6. National Drug Intelligence Center, "Methadone Diversion, Abuse, and Misuse," U.S. Department of Justice, November 2007. Available online. URL: http://www.justice.gov/ndic/pubs25/25930/25930p.pdf. Downloaded January 22, 2010.

7. National Drug Intelligence Center, "Executive Summary," National Prescription Drug Threat Assessment 2009. Available online. URL: http://www.usdoj.gov/ndic/pubs33/33775/

execsum.htm#Figure1. Downloaded January 20, 2010.

8. Office of Applied Studies, "Results from the 2008 National Survey on Drug Use and Health: National Findings," U.S. Department of Health and Human Services, Substance Abuse and Mental Health Services Administration. Available online. URL: http://www.oas. samhsa.gov/NSDUH/ 2k8NSDUH/2k8results. cfm#Ch2. Downloaded January 20, 2010.

9. Drug Policy Alliance Network, "911 Good Samaritan," drugpolicy.org. Available online. URL: http://www.drugpolicy. org/docUploads/NewMexico 911GoodSamaritanFactSheet. pdf. Downloaded January 21, 2010.

10. Drug Enforcement Administration, "State Prescription Drug Monitoring Programs," U.S. Department of Justice. Available online. URL: http://www. deadiversion.usdoj.gov/faq/rx_ monitor.htm#1. Downloaded January 21, 2010.

11. "Prescription Drug Monitoring Programs," National Conference of State Legislatures. Available online. URL: http://www.ncsl.org/default. aspx?tabid=12726. Downloaded January 21, 2010.

12. U.S. Drug Enforcement Administration, Controlled Substances Act. Available online. URL: http://www.usdoj. gov/dea/pubs/csa.html. Downloaded January 21, 2010.

Chapter 7

1. "What Can We Expect from Substance Abuse Treatment?" Centers for Disease Control. Available online. URL: http:// www.cdc.gov/idu/facts/ Expectations.htm. Downloaded January 18, 2010.

2. "What Every Parent Should Know About Drug Abuse in America," OHS Health & Safety Services, Inc. Available online. URL: http://www.ohsinc.com/ what_every_parent_should_ know_part2.htm/ Downloaded January 23, 2010.

3. OHS, "Cheating on a Drug Test Successfully Is Getting Tougher . . . ," Occupational Health & Safety Services, Inc.. Available online. URL: http:// www.ohsinc.com/cheat_ cheating_drug_tests.htm. Downloaded November 17, 2009.

4. Lisa M. Novak, "Navy Steps Up Drug Testing Program," *Stars and Stripes*. August 13, 2009. Available online. URL: http://www.military.com/ news/article/navy-steps-

up-drug-testing-program. html?ESRC=topstories.RSS. Downloaded November 17, 2009.

5. U.S. National Drug Control Strategy, "What Works: Effective Public Health Responses to Drug Use," Office of National Drug Control Policy. Available online. URL: http://www.ncjrs. gov/ondcppubs/publications/ pdf/whatworks.pdf. Downloaded January 23, 2010.

6. Nora D. Volkow, "What Can We Do?" NIDA Community Drug Alert Bulletin: Prescription Drugs, National Institute on Drug Abuse. Available online. URL: http://www.drugabuse.gov/ PrescripAlert/#what. Downloaded January 23, 2010.

7. James Vicini, "Supreme Court Rejects School Strip Search," Reuters, posted on June 25, 2009. Available online. URL: http://www. reuters.com/article/topNews/ idUSTRE55O48120090625. Downloaded January 22, 2010.

8. Yael Waknine, "FDA Approves Ibuprofen Injection to Treat Pain and Fever," Medscape Medical News, June 12, 2009. Available online with log-in. URL: http://www.medscape. com/viewarticle/704331. Downloaded January 23, 2010.

9. "Find the Latest Drug Product and Safety Information," U.S. Food and Drug Administration. Last updated November 10, 2009. Available online. URL: http://www.fda.gov/ ForConsumers/Consumer Updates/ucm107213.htm. Downloaded January 22, 2010.

10. "Medication Guides," U.S. Food and Drug Administration. Last updated January 13, 2010. Available online. URL: http://www.fda.gov/Drugs/ DrugSafety/ucm085729.htm. Downloaded January 22, 2010.

11. National Cancer Institute, "Magnetic Acupressure in Reducing Pain in Cancer Patients Undergoing Bone Marrow Aspiration and Biopsy," ClinicalTrials.gov, National Institutes of Health. Available online. URL: http:// www.clinicaltrials.gov/ct2/ show/NCT00670917?term=pa in+and+johns+hopkins&recr= Open&rank=13. Downloaded January 23, 2010.

12. MediLexicon International Ltd., "Electroacupuncture Shows Effects on Pain Perception," Medical News Today. Available online. URL: http:// www.medicalnewstoday.com/ articles/161233.php. Downloaded January 23, 2010.

13. Science News, "Acupressure Calms Children Before Surgery," ScienceDaily, October 2, 2008. Available online. URL: http://www.sciencedaily.com/releases/2008/10/081001130006.htm. Downloaded January 23, 2010.

14. Science News, "Therapy Helps Children and Teenagers in Pain," ScienceDaily, February 9, 2009. Available online. URL: http://www.sciencedaily.com/releases/2009/02/090204085303.htm. Downloaded January 23, 2010.

15. Aaron M. Gilson, "Laws and Regulations Governing Pain Relief with Opioids: Pain Policy Evaluation Resources," Medscape Neurology & Neurosurgery, published August 12, 2008. Available online with log-in. URL: http://www.medscape.com/viewarticle/577999_2. Downloaded January 23, 2010.

16. Center for Practical Bioethics, "Balanced Pain Policy Initiative," updated November 2007. Available online. URL: http://www.practicalbioethics.org/cpb.aspx?pgID=978. Downloaded January 23, 2010.

17. Stuart Wolpert, "Genetic Link Between Physical Pain and Social Rejection Discovered by Researchers," Medical News Today. Available online. URL: http://www.medicalnewstoday.com/articles/160995.php. Downloaded January 23, 2010.

Glossary

acetaminophen (Tylenol)   analgesic similar to aspirin or other nonsteroidal anti-inflammatory drugs (NSAIDs) but without the anti-inflammatory properties

acute pain   comes on quickly and can be severe but is usually treatable and does not last as long as chronic pain

addiction   disorder in which a person compulsively seeks and habitually uses drugs not to maintain health but rather in spite of the harmful effects this has on the body or mind

addictive   a drug having potential for chronic dependence

adverse event   an unexpected and often life-threatening reaction to a drug

alcohol   a natural product that occurs when fruit, vegetables, or grains ferment and which affects the central nervous system; also known as ethyl alcohol or ethanol

alkaloid   any of a number of natural organic, colorless, crystalline substances such as morphine, caffeine, and nicotine that are found in plants and that react with acids to form salts sometimes used for medical purposes

analgesic   commonly known as a painkiller but more precisely a pain blocker that hinders a hurt area from sending pain signals to the brain

anesthesia   drug given to numb pain during surgery

antidote   counteracting drug used to neutralize a toxin or poison

antihistamine   product used to combat the overproduction of natural histamines in the body when reacting to such allergens as dust, mold, foods, or insect bite

bradycardia   slow heartbeat and pulse rate

brain stem   links the brain to the spinal cord, moving muscles and letting the brain know what happens to the body

buccal   pertaining to the mouth or cheeks

buprenorphine semisynthetic opioid used to treat chronic pain; may be combined with naloxone to treat opioid addiction

cardiopulmonary resuscitation (CPR) lifesaving treatment that combines rescue breaths to help patients begin breathing on their own and chest compression to keep the heart beating and blood circulating until medical help can arrive

central nervous system the spinal cord and brain

cerebral cortex gray matter on the outer part of the brain that is divided into four areas, or lobes

chronic pain persistent pain that may not respond well to treatment

codeine the most commonly used opiate in the world; not as strong as morphine

complementary and alternative medicine (CAM) medical treatments and health products, such as acupuncture or herbal medicines, that derive from other than conventional Western medicine or methods

CPR See cardiopulmonary resuscitation

curative a tonic, elixir, herbal remedy, drug, or other medicine used to treat a medical condition or aid general health and well-being

cyclooxygenase (COX) a protein enzyme that causes NSAIDs to work

detoxify to withdraw from drug addiction, preferably with medical supervision; often shortened to "detox"

dopamine a neurotransmitter or messenger in the brain

drug abuse overuse of a prescription drug, use of a narcotic prescribed for someone else, or use of a prescription for something the doctor did not intend

drug dependence gradual adaptation to a drug so that the body experiences withdrawal symptoms without it

drug interaction occurs when certain medicines are combined, making drugs more dangerous or deadly

drug overdose accidental or intentional overuse of a narcotic, leading to coma, convulsions, or death

drug poisoning the body's reaction to ingestion of a toxic level of a drug; usually accidental but with the same potentially deadly results as an overdose when a sensitive patient reacts strongly to a medication

drug reaction a toxic or otherwise undesired response to medication

elixir   a sweetened liquid or other medicinal concoction usually containing alcohol

enzyme   proteins that cause changes in the body without being changed themselves

extract   the essential elements of a plant concentrated in juice, powder, or a solution often using alcohol

fentanyl   opioid used to treat both acute and chronic pain

forebrain   frontal cortex, or thinking center for the whole body

hemodialysis   a method of filtering the blood to remove toxins from the bloodstream; for instance, after a patient takes an excessive amount of aspirin

herbal medicine   a mixture using an extract or other part of an herb to help prevent or cure a medical condition

heroin   an illegal narcotic derived from morphine

hydrocodone bitartrate (Vicodin)   an analgesic drug

hydromorphone (Dilaudid)   a drug derived from morphine but less addictive and more stable, stronger, and faster in treating moderate to severe pain

hypodermic   a needle with a hollow tube and a plunger used to insert a fluid or medication in liquid form through a vein into the bloodstream

ibuprofen (Advil, Motrin, Nuprin)   a nonsteroidal anti-inflammatory drug (NSAID) that is available over the counter or in prescription strength

intravenous (IV) fluids   liquid injected into a vein to keep the cells of the body hydrated with water, minerals, and other vital nutrients

laudanum   a tincture of opium and alcohol developed in the early 1600s that became very popular during the Victorian era

levorphanol (Levo-Dromoran)   drug with pain relieving action stronger than morphine

limbic system   links brain structures that control emotional responses

lobes   four areas of the brain, each of which has a specific function

magnetic resonance imaging (MRI)   a diagnostic tool that uses electromagnetic energy to provide soft tissue images of the brain and central nervous system

meperidine hydrochloride (Demerol)   a narcotic analgesic

methadone   a synthetic narcotic used to ease withdrawal and treat addiction to opioids

migraine   occasional but severe headaches, usually on one side of the head, often accompanied by sensitivity to light and noise

morphine   a strong opioid that is used to treat severe pain even during surgery

naloxone   medication used to treat opioid addiction, often in combination with buprenorphine

naltrexone   a derivative of naloxone that is sometimes used to treat opioid addiction

narcotic   habit-forming drugs such as morphine, codeine, heroin, or opium that depress the central nervous system and ease pain. Although the term *narcotic* is still used by law enforcement agencies and others, medical personnel may mean the same thing when they refer to opioid analgesics.

neuralgia   pain along a nerve

neurotransmitter   a chemical messenger in the brain

nonsteroidal anti-inflammatory drug (NSAID)   an analgesic such as ibuprofen, aspirin, or acetaminophen available over the counter or in prescription strength

numeric pain scale   a standardized assessment whereby a medical professional asks a patient to rate the intensity of pain on a scale of 0 to 10 with 0 meaning no discomfort and 10 very severe pain

opiate   a drug extracted from ingredients in poppy pods to produce such natural but addictive drugs as morphine, codeine, and thebaine

opioid   the narcotic family of opiates, including natural, synthetic, and semi-synthetic forms of the drug

opioid analgesic   a pain-relieving narcotic apt to be habit-forming

opium   a strong narcotic naturally derived for thousands of years from the sap in the seed pods of the poppy plant

overdose   ingestion of too much of a drug or more than a body can handle, resulting in hysteria, coma, or death

over-the-counter (OTC) drugs   drugs that are available without a prescription

oxycodone (OxyContin, Percocet, Percodan, and Tylox)   strong opioid analgesics used for high pain relief that have a high potential for abuse

oxymorphone   group of habit-forming pain relievers similar to morphine

pain   usually classified as acute or chronic and rated on a scale from 0 to 10

pain management   various types of therapies or medications used to ease pain

palliative care   means of soothing, calming, or sedating a patient who has the severe chronic pain often associated with a terminal illness

paregoric   a liquid taken by mouth that contains alcohol, opium, and other ingredients used to treat diarrhea

pentazocine (Talwin)   opioid pain reliever similar to codeine

pharming   a dangerous social event where teens swap and mix drugs

physical dependence   a condition in which a person needs a drug for physical well-being

prescription drug monitoring   databases used by U.S. states to keep track of prescription medicines

propoxyphene (Darvon, Darvocet)   a group of narcotic pain relievers

protein   the basic component of all living cells

respiration   the breathing process vital for life; 12 to 20 breaths per minute is the average rate for teenagers and adults

respiratory depression   life-threatening condition caused by analgesics or other drugs that lower the rate of breathing to the point where not enough oxygen is provided to the lungs

self-medicate   to treat oneself with some kind of medication without asking a doctor

semisynthetic opioids   drugs processed from natural opiates to produce heroin (diamorphine), oxycodone, hydrocodone, dihydrocodiene, hydromorphone, oxymorphone, buprenorphine, etorphine, naloxone, and nicomorphine

side effect   an unwanted or unexpected result such as headache, vomiting, rash, difficulty breathing, or death caused by a toxic reaction to a medication or combination of drugs

street drugs   drugs bought illegally

suppository   small cylinder of a gel or soap-like substance containing medication that's usually inserted in the rectum

synapse   the space between neurons that neurotransmitters leap across

synthetic opioids   synthesized drugs such as methadone, pethidine (Demerol), fentanyl alfentanil, sufentanil, remifentanil, carfentanyl pentazocine, phenazocine, tramadol, and loperamide

synthesize   to process or chemically alter

thebaine   a poisonous alkaloid derived from opium

tolerance   when a person needs a higher dose of a drug to have the effect first felt

tonic   liquid preparation or drug meant to tone, invigorate, or restore the body to health

toxic   poisonous

"trail mix"   a variety of drugs tossed into a bowl or bag and served at drug parties

tramadol   a synthetic opioid used to treat moderate pain and neuralgia

vital organ   a major part of the body, such as the heart, liver, kidney, or lung, that is necessary to sustain life

further Resources

Books

American Chronic Pain Association. *ACPA Consumer Guide to Pain Medication & Treatment.* Rocklin, Calif.: ACPA, 2009.

Baggaley, Ann, ed. *Human Body.* New York: Dorling Kindersley, 2001.

Beers, Mark H., M.D., editor-in-chief. *The Merck Manual of Medical Information,* 2nd home edition. Whitehouse Station, N.J.: Merck Research Laboratories, 2003.

Cassell, Dana K., Robert C. Salinas, M.D., and Peter A.S. Winn, M.D. *The Encyclopedia of Death and Dying.* New York: Facts On File, 2005.

Griffith, H. Winter, M.D. *Complete Guide to Prescription & Nonprescription Drugs.* Revised and updated by Stephen Moore, M.D. New York: Penguin, 2008.

Sayler, Mary Harwell, and Arya Nick Shamie, M.D. *The Back and Spine Systems and Disorders.* New York: Facts On File, 2007.

Thomas, Clayton L., M.D., ed. *Taber's Cyclopedic Medical Dictionary.* 18th ed. Philadelphia: F.A. Davis, 1997.

Veague, Heather Barnett. *Cutting and Self-Harm.* New York: Chelsea House, 2008.

Articles

AMA. "Standards, Laws, and Regulations Addressing Pain Medications and Medical Practice," Report 6 of the Council on Science and Public Health (A-07). Available online. URL: http://www.ama-assn.org/ama/no-index/about-ama/18464.shtml. Downloaded September 17, 2009.

Budman, Simon H., Jill M. Grimes Serrano, and Stephen F. Butler. "Can Abuse Deterrent Formulations Make a Difference? Expectation and Speculation," *Harm Reduction Journal* 6, 8 (May 29, 2009): p. 8.

CRC Health Group. "Teen OTC & Prescription Drug Abuse," Aspen Education Group. Available online. URL: http://www.teenoverthecounterdrugabuse.com/otc-abuse-vs-addiction.html. Downloaded November 3, 2009.

Elliott, Eric T., Christopher A. Souder, Troy Privette, and William H. Richardson. "Teen prescription drug abuse: a national epidemic," *Clinician Reviews* 18, 11 (November 2008): p. 18(5).

NIDA InfoFacts. "Prescription Pain and Other Medications," National Institute on Drug Abuse. Posted June 2006. Available online. URL: http://www.nida.nih.gov/PDF/Infofacts/PainMed06.pdf. Downloaded October, 2009.

———. "Understanding Drug Abuse and Addiction," The Science of Drug Abuse and Addiction. National Institute on Drug Abuse. Last updated July 27, 2009. Available online. URL: http://www.drugabuse.gov/Infofacts/understand.html. Downloaded October 30, 2009.

Office of Communications and Public Liaison. "Pain: Hope Through Research," National Institute of Neurological Disorders and Stroke, NIH Publication No. 01-2406. Last updated August 3, 2009. Available online. URL: http://www.ninds.nih.gov/disorders/chronic_pain/detail_chronic_pain.htm#125133084. Downloaded September 9, 2009.

Office of National Drug Control Policy. "Prescription for Danger," National Drug Control Policy. Available online. URL: http://www.streetdrugs.org/pdf/rx_rpt_2008.pdf. Downloaded September 7, 2009.

Price, Lawrence H., M.D., ed. "Prescription Drug Abuse Linked to Increased Availability of Pain Meds," *The Brown University Psychopharmacology Update* 20, 2 (February 2009): pp. 1, 6.

Stephens, Everett, M.D. "Toxicity, Opioids," eMedicine, March 2, 2009. Available online. URL: http://emedicine.medscape.com/article/815784-overview. Downloaded October 31, 2009.

Thomas, Clayton L., ed. "Pain," in *Taber's Cyclopedic Medical Dictionary.* 18th ed. Philadelphia: F.A. Davis, 1997.

Volkow, Nora D., M.D. "Prescription Drug Abuse." Testimony before the Subcommittee on Criminal Justice, Drug Policy, and Human Resources Committee on Government Reform, U.S. House of Representatives, July 26, 2006. Available online. URL: http://www.hhs.gov/asl/testify/t060726a.html. Downloaded September 7, 2009.

Web Sites

Get the Facts
http://www.drugwarfacts.org/cms

National Center for Complementary and Alternative Medicine
http://nccam.nih.gov

National Health Information Center
http://www.health.gov/nhic

Office of National Drug Control Policy
http://www.whitehousedrugpolicy.gov

Parents: The Anti-Drug
http://www.theantidrug.com

PDRhealth, Physicians' Desktop Reference
http://www.pdrhealth.com/home/home.aspx

Streetdrugs.org
http://www.streetdrugs.org

U.S. Drug Enforcement Administration
http://www.usdoj.gov/dea/index.htm

U.S. Food and Drug Administration
http://www.fda.gov

Organizations

American Academy of Pain Medicine
4700 W. Lake Avenue
Glenview, IL 60025
(847) 375-4731
(847) 375-6429 (fax)
http://www.painmed.org
info@painmed.org

American Association of Poison Control Centers
3201 New Mexico Avenue
Suite 330

Washington, DC 20016
(800) 222-1222
http://www.aapcc.org/DNN
info@aapcc.org

American Chronic Pain Association
P.O. Box 850
Rocklin, CA 95677
(800) 533-3231
(916) 632-3208 (fax)
http://www.theacpa.org
ACPA@pacbell.net

American Pain Society
4700 West Lake Avenue
Glenview, IL 60025
(847) 375-4715
(866) 574-2654 or (847) 375-6479 (fax)
(732) 460-7318 (international fax)
http://www.ampainsoc.org
info@ampainsoc.org

National Foundation for the Treatment of Pain
P.O. Box 70045
Houston, TX 77270-0045
(713) 862-9332
(713) 862-9346 (fax)
http://www.paincare.org
jfshmd@gmail.com

National Institute of Neurological Disorders and Stroke
NIH Neurological Institute
P.O. Box 5801
Bethesda, MD 20824
(800) 352–9424 or (301) 496-5751
(301) 468-5981 (for people using adaptive equipment)
http://www.ninds.nih.gov
http://www.ninds.nih.gov/contact_us.htm

National Institute on Drug Abuse

National Institutes of Health
6001 Executive Boulevard
Room 5213
Bethesda, MD 20892-9561
(301) 443-1124
http://www.drugabuse.gov
information@nida.nih.gov

National Youth Antidrug Media Campaign

Drug Policy Information Clearinghouse
P.O. Box 6000
Rockville, MD 20849-6000
(800) 666–3332 or (800) 666–3332
(301) 519–5212 (fax)
http://www.mediacampaign.org/index.html
http://www.whitehousedrugpolicy.gov/utilities/contact_form.html

Partnership for a Drug-Free America

405 Lexington Avenue
Suite 1601
New York, NY 10174
(212) 922-1560
(212) 922-1570 (fax)
http://www.drugfree.org
http://www.drugfree.org/Portal/Contact

Substance Abuse and Mental Health Services Administration

Center for Substance Abuse Prevention/Family Guide
1 Choke Cherry Road
Rockville, MD 20857
(800) 789-2647 (to locate mental health resources)
(800) 729-6686 (to locate resources concerning substance abuse)
http://www.family.samhsa.gov
http://www.family.samhsa.gov/main/feedback.aspx

Index

About the Author

Mary Harwell Sayler has authored more than 25 books of fiction and nonfiction, including two life-health encyclopedias, *The Encyclopedia of the Muscle and Skeletal Systems and Disorders* and *The Encyclopedia of the Back and Spine Systems and Disorders* published by Facts On File. Besides her avid interest in researching almost any aspect of health, the author helps other poets and writers through her Web site The Poetry Editor and is herself a published poet, who often explores the poetic insights found in nature, including human nature and the many causes of pain.

About the Consulting Editor

Consulting editor **David J. Triggle, Ph.D.,** is a SUNY Distinguished Professor and the University Professor at the State University of New York at Buffalo. These are the two highest academic ranks of the university. Professor Triggle received his education in the United Kingdom with a Ph.D. degree in chemistry at the University of Hull. Following post-doctoral fellowships at the University of Ottawa (Canada) and the University of London (United Kingdom) he assumed a position in the School of Pharmacy at the University at Buffalo. He served as chairman of the Department of Biochemical Pharmacology from 1971 to 1985 and as Dean of the School of Pharmacy from 1985 to 1995. From 1996 to 2001 he served as Dean of the Graduate School and from 1999 to 2001 was also the University Provost. He is currently the University Professor, in which capacity he teaches bioethics and science policy, and is President of the Center for Inquiry Institute, a think tank located in Amherst, New York and devoted to issues around the public understanding of science. In the latter respect he is a major contributor to the online M.Ed. program—"Science and The Public"—in the Graduate School of Education and The Center for Inquiry.